Theology, Psychoanalysis, Trauma

The Veritas Series

Belief and Metaphysics
Edited by Conor Cunningham and Peter M. Candler, Jr

Proposing Theology
John Milbank

Tayloring Reformed Epistemology:
Charles Taylor, Alvin Plantinga and the de jure Challenge to
Christian Belief
Deane-Peter Baker

Theology, Psychoanalysis, Trauma
Marcus Pound

Transcendence and Phenomenology
Edited by Conor Cunningham and Peter M. Candler, Jr

VERITAS

Theology, Psychoanalysis, Trauma

Marcus Pound

scm press

© Marcus Pound 2007

British Library Cataloguing in Publication data

A catalogue record for this book is available
from the British Library

Hardback 978 0 334 04152 8
Paperback 978 0 334 4139 9

First published in 2007 by SCM Press
13–17 Long Lane,
London EC1A 9PN

www.scm-canterburypress.co.uk

SCM Press is a division of
SCM-Canterbury Press Ltd

Typeset by Regent Typesetting, London
Printed and bound in Great Britain by
MPG Books Ltd, Bodmin, Cornwall

Contents

Centre of Theology and Philosophy

www.theologyphilosophycentre.co.uk

Every doctrine which does not reach the one thing necessary, every separated philosophy, will remain deceived by false appearances. It will be a doctrine, it will not be Philosophy.
Maurice Blondel, 1861–1949

This book series is the product of the work carried out at the Centre of Theology and Philosophy, at the University of Nottingham.

The COTP is a research-led institution organized at the interstices of theology and philosophy. It is founded on the conviction that these two disciplines cannot be adequately understood or further developed, save with reference to each other. This is true in historical terms, since we cannot comprehend our Western cultural legacy unless we acknowledge the interaction of the Hebraic and Hellenic traditions. It is also true conceptually, since reasoning is not fully separable from faith and hope, or conceptual reflection from revelatory disclosure. The reverse also holds, in either case.

The Centre is concerned with:

- The historical interaction between theology and philosophy.
- The current relation between the two disciplines.
- Attempts to overcome the analytic/Continental divide in philosophy.
- The question of the status of 'metaphysics'. Is the term used equivocally? Is it now at an end? Or have twentieth-century attempts to have a post-metaphysical philosophy themselves come to and end?
- The construction of a rich Catholic humanism.

I am very glad to be associated with the endeavours of this extremely important Centre that helps to further work of enor-

mous importance. Among its concerns is the question whether modernity is more an interim than a completion – an interim between a pre-modernity in which the porosity between theology and philosophy was granted, perhaps taken for granted, and a postmodernity where their porosity must be unclogged and enacted anew. Through the work of leading theologians of international stature and philosophers whose writings bear on this porosity, the Centre offers an exciting forum to advance in diverse ways this challenging and entirely needful, and cutting-edge work. Professor William Desmond (Leuven)

VERITAS

Series Introduction

'. . . the truth will set you free.' (John 8.31)

Pontius Pilate said to Christ, 'What is truth?' And he remained silent. In much contemporary discourse, Pilate's question has been taken to mark the absolute boundary of human thought. Beyond this boundary, it is often suggested, is an intellectual hinterland into which we must not venture. This terrain is an agnosticism of thought: because truth cannot be possessed, it must not be spoken. Thus, it is argued that the defenders of 'truth' in our day are often traffickers in ideology, merchants of counterfeits, or anti-liberal. They are, because it is somewhat taken for granted that Nietzsche's word is final. truth is the domain of tyranny.

Is this indeed the case, or might another vision of truth offer itself? The ancient Greeks named the love of wisdom as *philia*, or friendship. The one who would become wise, they argued, would be a 'friend of truth'. For both philosophy and theology might be conceived as schools in the friendship of truth, as a kind of relation. For like friendship, truth is as much discovered as it is made. If truth is then so elusive, if its domain is *terra incognita*, perhaps this is because it arrives to us – unannounced – as gift, as a person, and not some thing.

The aim of the *Veritas* book series is to publish incisive and original current scholarly work that inhabits 'the between' and 'the beyond' of theology and philosophy. These volumes will all share a common aspiration to transcend the institutional divorce in which these two disciplines often find themselves, and to engage questions of pressing concern to both philosophers and theologians in such a way as to reinvigorate both disciplines with a kind of interdisciplinary desire, often so absent in contemporary academe. In a word, these volumes represent collective efforts in the befriending of truth, doing so beyond the simulacra of pretend tolerance, the violent, yet insipid reasoning of liberalism that asks with Pilate, What is truth? – expecting a consensus of non-commitment; one that encourages the commodification of the mind, now sedated by the civil service of career, ministered by the frightened patrons of position.

The series will therefore consist of two 'wings': 1, original monographs; and 2, essay collections on a range of topics in theology and philosophy. The latter will principally be the products of the annual conferences of the Centre of Theology and Philosophy (www.theologyphilosophycentre.co.uk).

Conor Cunningham
Peter Candler
Series editors

Preface

As I recall, it was not without some embarrassment that my catechist broached the doctrine of transubstantiation, or the claim that Christ is substantially present in the bread and wine offered up during the Sacred Mass. Such embarrassment seems to reflect a broad consensus today that it is somehow easier to believe that God created the world than that he changes bread and wine into Christ's actual body and blood. Perhaps because while a general belief in God is really not that out of the ordinary, sitting quite comfortably at the limits of the known world (the so-called god of the gaps), transubstantiation invites a particular belief, one that not only concerns an everyday event, but one wholly at odds with everything an empirical and rational mind has been brought up to believe.

Yet if one is allowed a favourite doctrine then transubstantiation is mine. Maybe because it remains such an affront to the senses, inviting a moment of unfathomable mystery into a world that increasingly refuses all that cannot be quantified and qualified by our senses; or perhaps because so much of Catholic identity and practice is tied up in this event: the Sacred Mass, veneration of host, down to features such as the colour of candles. But for whatever reasons the question remains: How does one speak of transubstantiation today, in the twenty-first century?

Of course, one can always simply appeal to tradition. Considered to have been a part of the early Church (Pohle, 1909, pp. 572–90) transubstantiation was formally ratified at the Fourth Lateran Council (1215): 'His body and blood are truly contained in the sacrament of the altar under the forms of bread and wine' (Tanner, 1990, p. 230) and reaffirmed at the Council of Trent (1545). The Second Vatican Council (1962–5) reaffirmed Trent: 'there is no other way in which Christ can be present except through the conversion of the entire substance of bread into his Body' (Flannery, 1982, p. 393) and the doctrine is maintained up to the present day in the *Catechism*: Christ is present '*in the Eucharistic species*' (§1373). In short the Church has resolutely maintained the identity of Christ with those sacramental elements beyond what may be taken as a mere act of remembrance. Hence to believe otherwise is already to be standing outside the tradition. Yet surely the Church has a responsibility to explain itself to the world into which it was born? After all, doctrine is not a private language game any more than language is private.

Historically, the appeal to an existing philosophical tradition was taken by that bastion of church orthodoxy, the angelic doctor Aquinas. Aquinas famously employed Aristotelian categories to account for the miracle. Drawing on the distinction between a thing's substance and accidents he argued that the bread and wine are transformed at the level of their substance (*essentia* or essence), but not their accidents (*esse* or existence) (ST III, q. 75, a. 5). Hence while the bread and wine still look and taste like bread and wine, the transition occurs on the metaphysical plane. And for good reason too; after all, who really wants to eat manifest human flesh and blood? But while Thomas may make sense of transubstantiation to those versed in Aristotle, to what extent does his invocation of the Philosopher speak to us today? To what extent can we uncritically assume an Aristotelian ontology to the Eucharist? My feeling is, not very well.

Are we therefore to abandon Aquinas? On the contrary, because, were he alive today, it is not Aristotle he would be engaging with, but more contemporary strains of thought, those associated with so-called postmodernism, since it is the postmodernists who not only present the greatest challenge to the intellectual life of the Church – the loss of grand narratives, death of self, and reduction of institutions to power – they define our cultural milieu. In other words, if we are to remain faithful to Aquinas it cannot be a matter of merely repeating him verbatim, but repeating his gesture and finding a contemporary voice in which to rearticulate this troubling doctrine.

The wager of this work is that if the Church is to communicate the mystery of transubstantiation within our cultural milieu, then psychoanalysis, and in particular Jacques Lacan's postmodern variation, provides the most coherent language. After all, psychoanalysis is today as Aristotle was to the Middle Ages, occupying a privileged place in contemporary thought, having taken root across the humanities in fields stretching from philosophy, politics, and theology to film studies. And neither has it been restricted to the academy. Freud's original ideas have seamlessly entered into common parlance – the Freudian slip, the Oedipal complex, unconscious repression. As the poet W. H. Auden famously put it, 'if often he was wrong and, at times, absurd/ to us he is no more a person/ now but a whole climate of opinion' (Auden, 1940). As for Lacan, no psychoanalyst has done more to rearticulate Freud within a postmodern sensibility, transposing Freud's early insights into the idiom of semiotics. Moreover, despite the obtuseness of his style, approximately half of the world's psychoanalysts employ his ideas in their clinical work (Hill, 2002, p. 11).

In drawing on Lacan there is one concept in particular that I believe speaks the mystery of the Eucharist, in terms of both the transformation that occurs *in* the bread and wine, and the transformative effect the bread and wine has *on* the participant: *trauma*. In short, the wager of this work is that transubstantiation is primarily a traumatic event and the eucharistic community a traumatic community.

Trauma – the language of psychoanalysis – brings the broken God-man to the fulcrum of the Mass as we are called to identify as participants and perpetrators of his traumatic death. Yet how often do we think of the Eucharist as a traumatic event? Consider by analogy how we have rendered safe and sterile the nativity scene: freshly plumped hay and unblemished linen, while in the wings animals look on with wonderment; yet

Christ was born amidst the shit and stench of the stables, like the lotus flower arising out of the mud, a symbol of beauty set against hardship and pain.* Perhaps then we need reminding of the trauma of the Eucharist, although not in the manner of Mel Gibson's recent film *The Passion of Christ*, a perverse fetishizing of violence with redemption tacked on. Because if the Church is to be a place of healing (not unlike the analyst's couch), then healing begins with the pain of confrontation. So if my argument is correct, the reader will cease to view the Eucharist in sterile and safe terms; less a neurotic defence against God, than the very place of dramatic and traumatic confrontation – because the Eucharist only works if God breaks (*trauma*) into time, *every* time, and it is not simply celebrated as an act of remembrance.

In developing my ideas through conferences and various conversations, I am often confronted by a look of incredulity followed by the question: Why on earth would anyone want to revitalize this obscurantist doctrine? But this misses the point, because what is at stake is not simply a nostalgia for a supernatural past, the kind of which pervades recent American shows such as *Buffy the Vampire Slayer* – although magical realism would be one way to describe the Sacred Mass – but rather the status of psychoanalysis, because a conversation is precisely *con*, that is with, and if theology is to risk mediating itself through a discourse that has traditionally been hostile towards it, then perhaps too psychoanalysis needs to risk itself; perhaps psychoanalysis may make itself intelligible through theological categories?

---

* I owe this insight to Gavin D'Costa.

Acknowledgements

It is axiomatic of Lacanian analysis that the analyst adopts the position of the Socratic midwife, maintaining a formal distance through measured interventions, thereby allowing the analysand to hear his unconscious desire. In arriving at this book, I am grateful to my 'analyst' and doctoral supervisor, Gavin D'Costa.

I would also like to acknowledge the University of Bristol and the Arts and Humanities Research Council for their financial assistance towards my PhD, out of which this book grew; to my parents Rose and Henry, I owe more than a debt of gratitude for their financial support; *grazie ai miei suoceri*, Antonietta e Marino whose use of the imperative: *mangia* saved me from too much study.

I also acknowledge the brilliance of Richard Johnson, whose passion for Kierkegaard and continued debate informed this work in a myriad of ways. For their help and advice in the process of gestation, I would like to thank especially Mario L. Beira, Eliana, Graham Ward, John Peacock, and Carolyn Wilde. Many have been those who have inspired and supported me towards the delivery of this book; among them I would like to record Nick Ansell, Tina Beattie, Emma Pound, Karen Kilby, Elizabeth O'Loughlin, Leigh Morgan and the Lacanian Bristol reading group. Thanks are also due to the staff at Bristol University's bookshop and library: Owen, Paul, and the indefatigable smile of Ann Legg. Special thanks also go to the friendship, generosity of vision, and constant encouragement of Conor Cunningham, and the trust of John Milbank.

According to Otto Rank, the primal experience of trauma is

birth, and the birth of this book has been no exception. More-over, like all births, it is the woman who principally suffers – in this case my wife, Eliana. During the process she has put up with my frustration, anxiety, enthusiasm, and even the odd tantrum; yet during that time her belief in the project has never wavered; indeed, more often than not, it has carried me. This book is dedicated her.

Guide to Abbreviations

Works by Freud

SE All references are to the *Standard Edition of the Complete Psychological Works of Freud*, 24 vols, ed. and trans. James Strachey, in collaboration with Anna Freud, assisted by Alix Strachey and Alan Tyson, London: Hogarth Press, 1953–74.

Works by Kierkegaard

AN 'Armed neutrality: or my position as a Christian author in Christendom', in *Point of View*, ed and trans. Howard V. Hong and Edna H. Hong, Princeton: Princeton University Press, 1998, pp. 127–41.

CA *The Concept of Anxiety*, trans. Reidar Thormte and Albert B. Anderson, Princeton: Princeton University Press, 1980.

CUP *Concluding Unscientific Postscript to Philosophical Fragments*, vols 1 and 2, ed. and trans. Howard V. Hong and Edna H. Hong, Princeton: Princeton University Press, 1992. All references will assume vol. 1 unless stated, for example (CUP 321) or (CUP 2:12).

E/O *Either/Or*, vols 1 and 2, ed. and trans. Howard V. Hong and Edna H. Hong, Princeton: Princeton University Press, 1987.

FSE 'For self-examination', in *For Self-Examination/Judge for Yourselves/Three Discourses*, trans. Walter Lowrie, London: Oxford University Press, 1941.

FT *Fear and Trembling/Repetition*, ed. Howard V. Hong and Edna H. Hong, Princeton: Princeton University Press, 1983.

JC *Philosophical Fragments/Johannes Climacus*, ed. and trans. Howard V. Hong and Edna H. Hong, Princeton: Princeton University Press, 1985.

JP *Journals and Papers*, vols 1–6, ed. and trans. Howard V. Hong and Edna H. Hong, London: Indiana University Press, 1967. The first number of the reference indicates the volume, the second the number given by Hong and Hong to the extract. For example (JP 3:2745).

MWA   'On my work as an author', in *The Point of View*, ed. and trans. Howard V. Hong and Edna H. Hong, Princeton: Princeton University Press, 1998, pp. 1–20.

PF   *Philosophical Fragments/Johannes Climacus*, ed. and trans. Howard V. Hong and Edna H. Hong, Princeton: Princeton University Press, 1985.

POV   *The Point of View*, ed. and trans. Howard V. Hong and Edna H. Hong, Princeton: Princeton University Press, 1998.

PA   'The present age', in *Two Ages: The Age of Revolution and the Present Age, a Literary Review*, ed. and trans. Howard V. Hong and Edna H. Hong, Princeton: Princeton University Press, 1978.

R   *Repetition*, in *Fear and Trembling/Repetition*, ed. Howard V. Hong and Edna H. Hong, Princeton: Princeton University Press, 1983, pp. 135–231.

SUD   *The Sickness Unto Death: A Christian Psychological Exposition for Upbuilding and Awakening*, ed. and trans. Howard V. Hong and Edna H. Hong, Princeton: Princeton University Press, 1980.

SLW   *Stages on Life's Way*, ed. and trans. Howard V. Hong and Edna H. Hong, Princeton: Princeton University Press, 1988.

TA   *Two Ages: The Age of Revolution and the Present Age, a Literary Review*, ed. and trans. Howard V. Hong and Edna H. Hong, Princeton: Princeton University Press, 197.

TC   *Training in Christianity*, trans. Walter Lowrie, Princeton: Princeton University Press, 1972.

WL   *Works of Love*, ed. and trans. Howard V. Hong and Edna H. Hong, Princeton: Princeton University Press, 1995.

Works by Lacan

E   *Écrits: A Selection*, trans. Bruce Fink, New York and London: W. W. Norton & Company, 2002. In a typical abbreviation (E 94/311), the second page reference is to the French edition, Jacques Lacan, *Écrits*, Paris: Seuil, 1966.

Éc   *Écrits*, Paris: Seuil, 1966.

PU   'Position of the unconscious' (1966), trans. Bruce Fink, in *Reading Seminar XI: Lacan's Four Fundamental Concepts of Psychoanalysis*, ed. Richard Feldstein, Bruce Fink, and Maire Jaanus, Albany: SUNY, 1995, pp. 259–82.

SI   *The Seminar of Jacques Lacan: Freud's Papers on Technique,*

Guide to Abbreviations

Be very sure not to understand the patient,
there is no surer way of getting lost. (SII 87)

Introduction

Theological engagement with psychoanalysis is by no means a recent phenomenon. Freud's work on religion invited immediate controversy. A self-proclaimed atheist, he famously located the origins of religious belief in an infantile state of humanity (SE 12:30). Like a small and helpless child who looks to the feared father for protection, early man, left to nature's whim, personified its fearful forces. By giving them the character of a father, man turned them into gods.

But Freud did not dismiss religion lightly. Being a wish-fulfilment, religion was not simply false, it satisfied a desire – the desire for protection. Religion therefore played a crucial societal role, a means to manage life in the face of nature's arbitrary whim. It was as Marx put it: opium for the people, that is, a medicine to relieve suffering. Moreover, with these newly fashioned gods, mankind could play out the Oedipal drama on a cosmic scale; the gods could be both feared and loved simultaneously like the father, thereby giving ritual and collective experience to that which we must all contend with as individuals.

What really troubled Freud therefore was not religion as such, but that religious truths were expressed mythically rather than scientifically, because like others of his day, Freud was a positivist: if a stable society were to emerge from war-torn Europe it would need to be established on sure and empirical foundations; and psychoanalysis would contribute to those foundations.

So Freud already conceived of psychoanalysis as a secular form of theology to the extent that both play a pivotal role in aligning us within the social space. And it too would confirm the truth of Christianity (and not Judaism): to enter social life one must pass through the dead father. The difference was that where religion reconciled civilization to external threats by creating gods, psychoanalysis did the job on an individual level, helping man to overcome the internal threats arising from one's instinctual life.

Strangely enough, churches, ministers, and theologians were only too happy to oblige Freud in his positivism. Crucial here were the post-war years. Doctors were able to apply their experience of psychotherapy and shell-shock to civilian problems; this in turn spurned a wealth of publications, and new doctors came to recognize the value of psychological training. In short, psychotherapy gained an air of respectability. Coupled with this was the ever-receding tide of religion, a loss of clerical confidence, and the advancing shores of secularism. Yet as some early pioneers like Frank Lake perceived, the new profession of psychotherapy was easily applicable to pastoral duties, offering 'credible ways of working usefully to facilitate human well-being' (Ballard, 2000, p. 65), thereby grounding the work of the Church in much-needed scientific credibility.

A psychiatrist by training, Lake found common cause between the analyst and pastor in their desire to understand humans in their extremities of suffering. Lake argued that pastors depended on behavioural and psychological insights which were 'common to all' (Lake, 1966, p. xxix). Psychotherapy could teach the pastor how to interview people, bear the pain of his own personality, deal with resistances, and so on; giving the pastor the practical skills and theoretical underpinning to legitimate and extend pastoral work to the most maladapted or disturbed members of society.

Lake's methods were controversial. He would often administer large doses of LSD to his patients and encourage the abreaction of painful childhood memories. Nonetheless, Lake was also a committed Christian and so the goal of pastoral care had to be not merely self-realization, but 'Christ-realization', and for this reason Lake gave a central role to sacramental life in the therapeutic process (Lake, 1966, p. xvi). The anamnesis one undergoes in therapy was to be supported by, and participate in, the central anamnesis of Christ in the Eucharist, such that self-realization becomes 'Christ-realization' and sacramental life the paradigm of therapy.

Arguably Lake was the first to understand that psychoanalysis needed to be practised within a participatory and liturgical framework – the argument of this book; yet if his work remains problematic it is not because of his liberal advocacy of LSD, but because in the end theology is subordinated to psychoanalysis and not the other way around. For example, salvation seems to care less about God than achieving an autonomous and secure ego which is to be supplemented with supernatural 'fortitude'. God appears as the religious equivalent of a body-builder's steroids, providing extra muscle to a more general course of well-being.

Theology and Secular Reason

Lake's problem arises because he assumes the ultimate autonomy of the secular sphere. Yet according to the work of John Milbank, the secular is not of itself a given reality, a space of the 'purely human' to be discovered once the cobwebs of superstition have been cleared away. Rather, the secular was *imagined* (Milbank, 1993, p. 9), discursively created through the emergent disciplines of the social sciences which are of themselves already bastardized forms of theology. Take natural law for instance. From the perspective of the political sciences natural law was no longer a means of mediating the divine, the basis of a participatory good. Instead, it was posited that humans, left to a state of nature, were self-seeking individuals whose sole motivation was the preservation of their own sphere of interest. Therefore, it was in their best interest to enter a mutual contract, curbing some of their rights at the expense of securing their sphere of influence. In this way the human subject was manifest within relations of pure immanence and the secular was constituted as a field of the formal power relations required to maintain the social order. What remained of religion was deemed utterly private, transcendent, and ineffable and as such banished from the social, thereby confirming the autonomy of the secular (Milbank, 1993, pp. 9–12).

Yet, as Milbank argues, theology *is* a social theory, one that seeks to promote mutual social relations, without being predicated upon the notion of the private individual or need to formally exercise power; but of neighbourly love, spontaneous charity, and learnt virtue; and if it fails to challenge the autonomy of the secular it will inevitably be positioned by it, reduced to an immanent field of knowledge such as wish-fulfilment, or tucked away in some private ineffable realm.

It is not difficult to extend Milbank's project to psychoanalysis. After all, psychoanalysis was key in securing at the level of the individual what was posited of the social. Early interpreters of Freud such as his daughter Anna, Harry Guntrip, or Heinz Hartmann, all argued that the self was in origin a bundle of self-seeking drives, the primary expression of nature, a chaos which needed to be brought into social conformity through the rationalizing principle of the ego – the approach known as ego-psychology.[1] And like Hobbes, man would pass from nature to society through a contractual agreement; only now the contractual agreement specifically targets the sexual relation: the

---

[1] For a brief overview of ego-psychology see Harold P. Blum, 'Ego-psychology and contemporary structural theory', *International Psychoanalysis* 2 (1998), http://www.ipa.org.uk/newsletter/98-2/blum1.htm and David Rapaport, 'A historical survey of psychoanalytic ego-psychology', *Psychological Issues* 1. 1 (1959), pp. 5–17. Rapaport discerns four stages. The first stage coincides with Freud's pre-psychoanalytic writings where he initially sketches the ego in relation to defence and reality. The second stage ends in 1923 with the development of psychoanalysis proper, the collapse of the seduction theory and elaboration of drives. The third phase begins with Freud's second topography outlined in *The Ego and the Id*. The fourth stage is signalled by the work of Hartmann and his collaborators who developed Freud's theory of the ego.

ban upon incest. Moreover, like the social contract, it affords a certain compromise: one may not have exactly what one wants (i.e. the mother); nonetheless, one can always find a respectable substitute. Psychoanalysis was therefore a profoundly conservative project, aimed at helping the subject adjust to a reality defined in advance by wider secular and political thought. And it is perhaps for this reason that should theology fail to assume a meta-critical stance apropos psychoanalysis, it will inevitably be positioned by it, confined to existing social reality. Salvation will become indistinguishable from achieving a secure ego-identity, and the Church's ability to speak out against wider political and economic injustice will be seriously compromised.

It is not my intention to provide a genealogy of psycho-analysis in the manner of Milbank on sociology, but rather to engage psychoanalysis from a theological and meta-critical stance, to explore the way psychoanalysis is already a theology and thereby encourage theology to think of itself as already psychology, and liturgy *as* psychoanalysis.

Psychoanalysis and Postmodernism

In engaging psychoanalysis, I look in particular at postmodern psychoanalysis. My reasons are twofold. First, most theological engagement with psychoanalysis has, as I argue shortly, engaged with a particular school of psychology: ego-psychology. The result is that salvation is understood in terms of securing a strong and autonomous ego-identity which must adjust to a reality defined in advance. Second, postmodern psychoanalysis represents a major shift in assumptions. Where Freud situated the psyche within biology, postmodern psychoanalysis situates the psyche almost entirely within language. One can discern the importance of this shift most clearly in the status of the ego. Whereas the early Freudians take the ego as the locus of the self, and accordingly its principal aim to secure the ego against internal drives while adapting it to external reality, postmodern psychoanalysis considers the ego an illusion. The self is a construct of language, and identity as arbitrary and shifting as the language it is built upon. Hence the aim of analysis is to expose the illusion of the ego, reconciling one to the ceaseless flux of language and absence of an interior grounding.

Rather than see this as antithetical to theology, the final effacement of man by language, and second only to the death of God, I argue that they are values and concepts that have been actively promoted by theologians to the extent that the shift from modern to postmodern psychoanalysis marks a major shift towards a more mutual engagement between theology and psychoanalysis.

Lacan and Kierkegaard

In bringing psychoanalysis into dialogue with theology, I take as my principal dialogue partners the analyst Jacques Lacan (1901–81), and the theologian Søren Kierkegaard (1813–55). Lacan is famous for his 'return to Freud', rewriting Freudian psychology on the basis of structural linguistics. For Lacan, it is as if everything Freud said was absolutely true, only he was really talking about language. For example, castration does not bear on the biological penis – the fear of losing (male) or of already having lost (female) an anatomical organ; castration is an effect of language, the inability of us to be the object of desire for the mother due to the economy of ever-shifting linguistic signs. Likewise, the Oedipal complex is really a story explaining how we enter language, that is, law, because language structures all human relations. And accordingly, the unconscious is not a localized space where repressed thoughts are to be found; it is there in our language, in the garbled words, slipped tongues, and sheer profusion of meaning that the ceaseless play of language forces upon us.

Kierkegaard by contrast was a Danish theologian. His tirades against Christian nominalism and the wild abstractions of Hegelian or speculative philosophy, as he called it, were motivated by a profound sense that Christianity was primarily a lived experience. What matters is not the objective status of Christianity (for example: Was Christ really God?), but whether one manifests one's life as a lived expression of that truth (that is, one is obedient to Christ because he is God). Christianity *is* the God-relation, a relation for which the subject must take responsibility and existentially manifest through absolute commitment.

It might appear initially that Lacan and Kierkegaard are diametrically opposed. After all, Lacan is an affirmed atheist while Kierkegaard is a fideist theologian. Moreover, what we find in Lacan is the subject both situated and created within the diffusion of language; a subject for whom there is no underlying self-identity and no basis for agency. In contrast, the Kierke-gaardian subject is grounded in agency and affirmation to the point where Kierkegaard has been accused of an extreme indi-vidualism (MacIntyre, 1999, p. 52).

This is certainly the view presented by David Crownfield, who, concluding a collection of theological essays on Lacan, draws a contrast between the alienated subject described by Lacan, and the Kierkegaardian subject who becomes a self in the moment of faith: dissemination (Lacan) versus decision (Kierkegaard) (Crownfield, 1989). He points out that if we are to follow Kierkegaard, the issue of selfhood is resolved in the decision of faith. By contrast, if we are to take up Lacan's thought, it is only by bringing the 'centrelessness of life, the incoherence of self' (Crownfield, 1989, p. 162) to speech that the issue of selfhood can be treated properly. Crownfield claims that these two views are absolutely incompatible: seen from Kierkegaard's perspective, Lacan's account of alienation is a strategy to avoid grounding the self in the absolute power – God. By situating the subject in the flux of language Lacan avoids the moment of decision. Meanwhile seen from Lacan's perspective, Kierkegaard's attempt to decisively ground the self in God simply spells alienation and is comparable with the mirror stage: God is invoked to offer a false sense of unity to the fragmented subject. Nonetheless, Crownfield concludes: 'Only in the plurality of evaluations of the discourse of the church and of Kierkegaardian issues of coherence of self could the problematic of Lacan and theological discourse usefully be explored' (Crownfield, 1989, p. 169); that is to say, Lacan and Kierkegaard stand at the parameters of any discussion on subjectivity.

In a typically Lacanian fashion one should assert that when things seem most apart they are often closest together – Christ being the ultimate example of this: he is a God precisely because he is the only person who is fully human. Hence I argue that while Lacan considers the self a redundant concept, he nonetheless allows for a strong sense of agency and affirmation, thereby bringing him into proximity with Kierkegaard. Likewise while Kierkegaard emphasizes the need for existential responsibility and asserting the self through a conscious decision, he too recognizes the profound ways in which selfhood is fragmented by language, dispersed, and displaced by the signifier, and in many cases presupposes Lacan's central insights about subjectivity. In the following chapters I intend to tease out Kierkegaard and Lacan's alternative sides, and make good on Crownfield's suggestion that the dialogue between psychoanalysis and theology take place between these two figures.

Lacan and Theology

Lacan is no stranger to theology. In rewriting Freud from the perspective of structural linguistics, he updates Freud's critique of religion. For example, in *Seminar VII* he says 'religion in all its forms' (SVII 130) is an attempt to avoid the constitutive lack of being (*das Ding*). In other words, religion arises out of a need to defend ourselves against the anxiety of the real. Moreover, in referring to the relations between religion and psychoanalysis, he says:

> [they] are not very amicable. In sum, it is either one or the other. If religion triumphs as is most probable – I speak of the true religion and there is only one which is true [i.e. Roman

Catholicism] – if religion triumphs, this will be the sign that psychoanalysis has failed. (Richardson, 1986, p. 75)

Why does Lacan think that religion will triumph over psycho-analysis? Because religion is 'capable of giving a meaning, one can say, to anything at all – a meaning to human life for example' (Richardson, 1986, p. 75); yet meaning implies unity, and the singular feature of the unconscious is discontinuity. This is the form in which it [*Das Es*] appears: a forgotten word or a slip of the tongue, a bungled action or break in the normal flow of speech; what Freud called the parapraxis, an 'Act whose explicit goal is not attained; instead this goal turns out to have been replaced by another one' (Laplanche and Pontalis, 1988, p. 300). No wonder Lacan was wary of religion; to posit God as the *causa sui* risks drowning life in meaning. It would, as William Richardson says, close the chain of signification in upon a centre which would hold the signifier and signified together to become the absolute foundation of meaning (Richardson, 1997, p. 11).

It would appear then that Lacan offers little advance on Freud, defining religion as a form of neurosis. However, while appearing dismissive, he arguably maintains a more nuanced approach. For example, Lacan refers to the Oedipal prohibition against incest and murder as the Name-of-the-Father [*Nom-du-Père*]. In French, a pun is employed because 'name' and 'no' are anonyms, they are pronounced: '*nom*'. In this way he empha-sizes how the prohibition 'No!' occurs with language, that is, a name (in a similar fashion, rites of passage are often accompa-nied by awarding the child a new name as in the case of a Bar Mitzvah or confirmation). But the term is also the first line of the blessing, '*In the name of the Father*'; and just as the blessing inaugurates or configures particular spaces, so too submitting to the name provides for the collective ritual experience of language. So while Lacan reduces religion to language, he also raises language to the level of the religious. God, the big absence, plays the part of the big Other whose very lack becomes the condition of everything getting going in the first place (*creation ex nihilo*). And it is for this reason he is happy to defend the mystic St John of the Cross *against* the charge that St John's experiences were the delusional experiences of a psychotic. What makes him a genuine mystic is that he occupies the symbolic, that is, his work allows for a shared and creative engagement in the symbolic structures that govern human relations (SIII 77–8). So again, like Freud, Lacan already thought of psychoanalysis as a secular form of theology. Indeed, in a letter to his brother Marc-François, a Benedictine monk, Lacan asks that his brother intercede with papal authorities in the hope of gaining Catholic approval and thereby doing 'homage to our common Father' (Roudinesco, 1999, p. 205).

Despite this, it was not until *Lacan and Theological Discourse* (Wyschogrod et al., 1989) that the first major collection of essays by theologians on Lacan appeared. For many of these early interpreters like Mark C. Taylor and Charles Winquist, Lacan was primarily to be situated in a line of thinkers extending from Kierkegaard to Derrida who were critical of a systematizing and objectifying approach to life. Their climate distinctly belonged to Heidegger – they strove to think God from the perspective of ontological difference rather than the onto-theological *causa sui*; and they took their orientation from Derrida who had already made the connection between his own philosophy of différance, deferment and absence, with the tradition of negative theology in his essay 'How to Avoid Speaking: Denials' (Derrida, 1992, pp. 72–143).

For these writers Lacan was primarily to be taken as a psychoanalytic supplement to Derrida and 'an ally of theology' because like Derrida he 'forces theology to seriously assess the problematic of its own textuality', providing a philosophical reminder that theological discourse is a form of speech and it therefore speaks a lack (Winquist, 1989, p. 32). This reading of Lacan is then neatly coupled with the biblical rejoinder that one should not commit idolatry so as to create, as Catherine Clément puts it,

a miss-tical *a*/theology, one that would involve real risks. . . .
For Lacanian analysis 'does not provoke any triumph of self-
awareness' as Roudinesco rightly points out. 'It uncovers on
the contrary, a process of decentring, in which the subject
delves . . . into the loss of his mastery'. (Clément, 1983,
p. 144)

By ceding mastery, theology could become less concerned
with defending existing doctrine, and joins the chorus of
postmodern critiques against Enlightenment totalitarianism;
theology could become primarily a practice, and an 'ethical
experiment in letting things be in their otherness' (Winquist,
1989, p. 31).

However, the problem with this initial approach is twofold.
First, as David Crownfield suggests, all this undue emphasis
on a subject which is dispersed through the play of the signifier
precludes any type of 'Kierkegaardian affirmation as well as
more traditional forms of theology' (Crownfield, 1989, p. 163).
In other words, one risks starving theology of any positive content. And indeed, this is confirmed in the writing of Winquist
when he says of a post-Lacanian theology:

[it] would not be defined by the object of its enquiry. What
was in the centre of theological thinking and why theology
was itself in the centre of intellectual enquiry is now marked
by a lack and a loss. (Winquist, 1989, pp. 30–1)

Such an opinion echoes that of Mark C. Taylor. For Taylor,
the shift to postmodernism heralds a 'carnivalesque comedy' in
which God is dead, the incarnated Christ becomes ceaselessly
disseminated (Taylor, 1984, p. 163), and the subject undergoes
what Taylor, referring to Lacan, calls '*aphanisis* (the disappearance or obliteration of the subject by desire)' (Taylor, 1984,
p. 143). Taylor is not uncritical of Lacan. He argues that
Lacan's designation of Law in terms of the Name-of-the-Father
perpetuates patriarchy. Instead, he reads Nietzsche's death-of-
God as an end to the rule of the Father. Significantly, he draws

on Lacan's seminar 'God and Woman's *jouissance*' (SXX 64–77), where Lacan suggests there must be a specifically female *jouissance* not prey to the economy of patriarchy. Taylor suggests that an end to law will open up a space for the goddess to arise: 'To approach the goddess, one must refuse the refusal of the bar [Law]. Such refusal is always transgressive. The space of transgression is created by the bars that open' (Taylor, 1989, p. 50). The problem with Taylor's criticism is that he fails to take into account the role of law – be it the Father or otherwise – in separating the child from the mother. The removal of this bar can only condemn the child to the suffocating love of the mother, or the anxiety of never knowing quite what one is qua the mother's desire.

The lack of any institutional theology in Taylor and Winquist's work paints a picture of a very private and liberal theology, a criticism summed up well by Crownfield: these theologians 'locate theological discourse in the . . . imaginary, in the isolation of the solitary and marginal wanderer without context or community' (Crownfield, 1989, p. 38). By reading Lacan in this way theology is sublimated into the wider project of liberal modernity with its concomitant call for an autonomous individuality and privatized religion. And because religion is now under the private jurisdiction of the believer, despite their concern for Otherness, it would seem that a hidden form of mastery is smuggled in.

The second problem arises because these philosophers and theologians fail to take Lacan seriously as a clinician, treating him instead as a psychoanalytic complement to Derrida, in that he reminds us of a more fundamental philosophical principle about the diffusion and dissemination of meaning. Yet arguably the clinical setting is crucial to contextualizing his work because clinical practice defined his career. From 1927 to 1931 Lacan studied the clinical treatment of mental and cephalic disorders at the Hôpital Sainte-Anne, going on to work at the Special Infirmary of the Préfecture de Police and the Henri Rousselle hospital, as well as studying at the Burghölzli clinic in Zurich (Roudinesco, 1999, p. 17). Simply put, through the art of psychoanalysis, Lacan was committed to helping patients – or as he liked to refer to them, analysands[2] – and hence his seminars, directed towards analysts in training, never err from the clinical question: What is psychoanalysis, and how should it be practised?

To appreciate this need to contextualize Lacan's work clinically, consider the theme of ethics. Philosophical treatment alone tends to turn Lacanian ethics into an ethics of Otherness, an injunction against the idolatry of the ego and indeed all of life's little reifications. Yet what matters from the clinical perspective is the problem the analysand approaches the analyst with, coupled with the desire for change. Hence ethics concerns precisely the ability of that analysand to act in conformity with his desire to change. It is not enough for the analysand to speak his desire; he must manifest it through embodied action. Hence Lacan says of the ethics: 'it is a question of the relationship between action and desire, and of the former's failure to catch up with the latter' (SVII 313), and a little later on: 'Have you acted in conformity with the desire that is in you?' (SVII 314). What emerges is less a pathological fear of representation than a need for agency and decision.

Thus, in a bizarre twist, those theologians who adopt Lacan in the interest of a postmodern ethics of difference risk the very form of exclusion they seek to avoid *on* Lacan. As Safouan points out, in 1963 the International Psychoanalytic Association (IPA) agreed to recognize the Société Psychoanalytique de France (SFP), of which Lacan was a member, but only on the condition that the SFP expelled Lacan (Safouan, 2000, p. 2), thereby refusing to legitimize his clinical practice. Therefore, to continue to overlook the clinical context of Lacan's work as some philosophers are inclined to do is to inadvertently collude with the very forces he spent his life fighting against.

---

2 Lacan uses the gerund form of analyse to refer to the one who is 'in' analysis as a way to highlight their active participation in the process (Evans, 1996, p. 9).

Kierkegaard and Psychoanalysis

Kierkegaard's work on anxiety, his astute observations on personality types, and the eccentricity of his own life, have made him a popular source for psychologists. Existential therapists such as Ludwig Binswanger, Rollo May, and Victor Frankl were all indebted to his foundational work on anxiety, the cornerstone of existential psychology. Karen Horney drew on him in developing her own diagnostic categories, and Hans Loewald tried to give a more sympathetic reading of religion by engaging Freud and Kierkegaard's concept of repetition (Loewald, 1971, pp. 59–65). Lacan himself makes several references to Kierkegaard, usually in the context of the repetition compulsion, but also concerning Kierkegaard's work on seduction. Others have been more content to pathologize Kierkegaard, variously diagnosing him in terms of masochism-sadism, neurosis of obedience, manic-depressive, pathological melancholy, homosexuality (Taylor, 1975, n. 47), schizoid (Friedmann, 1949, p. 23), and epileptic (Garff, 2005, p. 460).

Of the early existential therapists Ernest Becker most notably engaged Kierkegaard directly. Becker had been influenced by Kierkegaard's description of dread as freedom's possibility awoken through the anxiety of death. One is anxious precisely to the extent one realizes that in life we can choose to be anything, and yet one *must* choose, that is, one must take absolute responsibility for one's life; and death impresses upon the individual the need to take responsibility. In *The Denial of Death* (1997) Becker argued that the anxiety of death had all but disappeared, and with that the loss of a certain type of human hero: the man of courage and dignity who believed in his own self-worth – a man prepared to act in the service of God rather than men. Becker argued that Kierkegaard's merger of religious and psychiatric categories seemed to offer the most acute analysis of the human condition as well as an antidote in the form of spiritual and existential responsibility, thereby replacing Freud's emphasis on sex with an awareness of death and temporality in the service of a higher reality.

But the problem arises because the Kierkegaard in question is said to extol the virtues of an 'ego-controlled and self-confident appraisal of the world' (Becker, 1997, p. 72). In other words, Kierkegaard is sublimated into an ego-psychology so that salvation amounts to having a healthy executive ego. But as I argue, this is a one-sided reading of Kierkegaard, because while agency is clearly important, Kierkegaard also remains someone for whom the self is fractured by language; someone who, besieged by the terror of freedom, must make a gesture that is of itself meaningless, because it is directed towards a God that is ultimately Other; and for whom human and divine speech is equally metaphorical and therefore contingent (WL 209–10).

In a less ambitious project focusing on Kierkegaard's pseudonyms, Mark C. Taylor also compared Kierkegaard's work to Freud's clinical structures. Examining in detail Kierkegaard's stages, Taylor concluded in each case that they represent not only ideal personality types, but stages in the maturation of the individual that anticipate much of Freudian/post-Freudian psychology. For example, the aesthetic stage where one is governed by the passions corresponds to the oral stage in which the pleasure principle dominates; the ethical stage corresponds to the late anal and early genital stage because this is the stage that law is introduced (potty training). Of the Christian stage Taylor writes:

At the Christian stage of existence Kierkegaard argues that the self achieves the balance within itself that has been the goal of the entire quest of self. The psychological phenomenon that he here isolates for consideration is what later students of personality called 'ego-integration.' It is the achievement of a genuine stability within the personality system that accompanies the development of the mature self. The psychologist calls this the achievement of a healthy self; the theologian, Kierkegaard, calls it the attainment of salvation. But the phenomenon being described is the same. (Taylor, 1975, p. 74)

Taylor's attempt to correlate the two concludes in a similar fashion to Becker, drawing the comparison between the healthy ego expounded by ego-psychology, and Kierkegaard's view of salvation or selfhood. But his work also highlights a further problem in that he paints a monological picture of Kierkegaard's authorship, organizing them into a developmental psychology. One gradually matures through a series of set stages to a point where having taken control of oneself one attains a consistency of selfhood. Yet Kierkegaard's use of pseudonyms plays out at the level of his readers what he posits of the self: that it is fractured, split, decentred, and dependent upon language; in short, riddled with inconsistencies. And likewise, the pseudonyms are to be read like this, as a variety of fractured encounters, as so many case studies which, as Amy Hall says, force us to 'peer inward at the multiple, often dubious motives propelling our own engagements, confess with dismay the irreparable fracture running through our love, and seek redemption' (Hall, 2002, p. 1).

Reading Kierkegaard this way, the emphasis falls not on an act of radical self-assertion, but, as Gillian Rose points out, an equal act of radical *dispossession* in the movement of a faith (Rose, 1992, p. 148), just as for Abraham making an absolute commitment in faith to God meant in that precise moment relinquishing his will; but more than that, because for Kierkegaard the divine is absolutely transcendent, and so the act of religious commitment entails that one relate all of one's life to something that remains utterly unknown and without common measure between the two. And so religion does not invite certainty; rather, it asks people to let go of the very last and reasonable thing they are holding onto. As one pseudonym says, 'no one on earth or in heaven knows, what danger is and what it is to be in danger as does the religious person, who knows that he is always in danger' (SLW 470).

The most sustained approach to Freud and Kierkegaard is Preston Cole's *The Problematic Self in Kierkegaard and Freud* (1971). Cole's thesis is that Freudian analysis is limited by its naturalistic framework which provides a deterministic model for selfhood. Through a comparative study that illuminates Kierkegaard's proximity to Freud he argues that Kierkegaard meets Freud's deficiencies by introducing a historical ontology, by which he means that Kierkegaard places first and foremost the category of becoming.

This is a largely comparative exercise. In bringing the two together, Cole believes that the therapist's paradigm refocuses Kierkegaard's theology as a historically embedded theology of becoming that orientates one towards a biblical faith; and this is to be contrasted to the theology of Karl Barth, for whom God's wholly otherness is privileged at the expense of his presence (Cole, 1971, p. 221).

However, it seems that biblical faith is not so important after all when Cole suggests that 'In Kierkegaard's concept of the self, an ego-psychology is posited' (Cole, 1971, p. 208), and thus selfhood for Kierkegaard amounts to, in Freudian terms, the healthy administration of the ego in its mediating role. So, despite wishing to retain a theology of sin and salvation, these are subtly brought into tension with a view that casts the restoration of selfhood in terms of the 'executive function' of the ego (Cole, 1971, p. 208).

In *Faith and Human Transformation* (1997) the Catholic writer James Forsyth explores the parallels between faith and psychoanalysis as transformative experiences. His two axiomatic principles are taken from Aquinas: *gratia praesupponit naturam* (grace presupposes or builds on nature) and *gratia perficit naturam* (grace perfects nature). Forsyth argues that human transformation serves as the basis for religious transformation and that grace presupposes or builds on nature. These relations provide the basis for an engagement between psychoanalysis (nature) and theology (grace). For example, drawing on the ideas of Donald Evans he suggests that 'the psychosocial ego-strengths become the natural foundation and experiential root of religion and morality' (Forsyth, 1997, p. xvi). That is to say, grace presupposes a degree of 'maturity' where maturity is defined in the terms of 'ego-strength' (Forsyth, 1997, p. xvii).

Cole and Forsyth further highlight that where Kierkegaard is brought into dialogue with psychoanalysis it is in the service of an ego-psychology. Lacan tirelessly critiqued ego-psychology and so the chance to reread Kierkegaard in the light of Lacan will help to address that literature. I argue that those psychologists and theologians were profoundly mistaken in their psychoanalytical appropriation of Kierkegaard. Indeed, I dare to make the original claim that Kierkegaard has far more in common with the postmodern meta-psychology of Lacan than ego-psychology, and hence Lacan's return to Freud can be read as a return to theology.

Methodology

The form of my argument is no simple comparison and conclusion. Nor do I intend to treat systematically Lacanian references to Kierkegaard. Rather, I perform, in a manner outlined in Chapter 2, an analytic intervention on Lacan. That is to say, just as analysis aims to illuminate the subject's speech in new ways through the use of interpretive interventions, I aim to enable Lacan to be read in a new way, through Kierkegaard. In short, I perform a Lacanian intervention on Lacan by way of Kierkegaard with a view to teasing out the hidden presuppositions, the underlying premises, and hence Lacan's disavowed truth, thereby making the Lacanian aware through Kierkegaard that Lacanian psychoanalysis is profoundly theological.

Another way to put this, using the language of Kierkegaard, is to say that my aim is to *repeat* Lacan. For Kierkegaard, as I explain in Chapter 3, there can be no repetition of the same, a literal rearticulation of what went before; such a movement is precluded by our engagement in time. For example, we cannot go backward or forward to relive an experience in exactly the same manner as before; however, it is possible to repeat what has been in a different form, that is, to repeat the difference that the initial experience made. For example, one cannot repeat verbatim the October revolution of 1918; nonetheless one can repeat the gesture to the extent one induces a similar traumatic cut in the life of a nation; that is, one repeats the original precisely through a difference.

I suggest that repetition is the basis of Lacan's rereading of Freud. Lacan does not repeat Freud verbatim; he does not simply rearticulate Freudian doctrine. Rather, by transposing Freud's work into the key of post-structural linguistics Lacan 'releases its [Freud's] significance for the present' (Kay, 2003, p. 19). What we encounter in Lacan is the same radical reasoning that was initially encountered in Freud, an affirmation of what went before, yet also an orientation to what might be. Lacan *repeats* Freud, through the difference he introduces. As Kay points out, the Slovenian philosopher Slavoj Žižek has performed a similar move on Hegel, rereading Hegel on the basis of Lacan. Žižek *repeats* Hegel, that is to say he releases Hegel's significance for the present, preserving a relationship of identity through its very difference, arguing that Lacan is the true heir of German Idealism. For example, Žižek argues that Hegel's thesis 'spirit is bone' is a precursor to Lacan's view of subjectivity ($S \lozenge a$). The skull is the object that fills out the void around which the subject coalesces, the positive form of the body's failure to fully represent itself to itself. So, just as for Lacan the subject's impossibility is the condition of its possibility (the subject must give up a portion of itself – being – to ascend to the symbolic – meaning), so for Hegel, the leftover portion of the real is bone to which Spirit is correlative (Žižek, 2002, pp. 201–9).

In a similar fashion it is my aim to repeat both Lacan and Kierkegaard, by transposing the work of each into the key of the other. I reread Kierkegaard on the basis of Lacan, thereby releasing Kierkegaard's significance for psychoanalysts, and repeat Lacan, reading him on the basis of Kierkegaard. In this way I argue that Lacan is the true heir of theology and Kierkegaard of psychoanalysis.

Returning to the idiom of Lacan, one could speak of this repetition in terms of deferred action [*nachträglich*]. What is at stake in deferred action – or to use a literal translation of the French, the after-cut – is the retroactive reconfiguration of what went before. Psychoanalytic time does not follow an uncritical construal of time as a long chain of events in which the present follows on from the past; rather, the past is heir to the present. As Lacan explains, given an event in the present, 'It's not what happens afterwards which is modified, but everything that went before. We have a retroactive effect – *nachträglich*, as Freud calls it' (SII 185). For Lacan this temporal paradox is the structure of a sentence. For example, the meaning of a sentence does not flow from the beginning to the end; rather, it is only when the end of a sentence is reached that one can make sense of the beginning. Likewise, my attempt is to perform an after-cut on Lacan, to retroactively reconfigure Lacan's critical roots, reconfiguring psychoanalysis so it becomes theology; and theology psychoanalysis. Indeed, as Lacan says, the reconfiguration of the past entails making it 'pass into the *verbe* [Logos], or more precisely, into the *epos* [speech, tale, song, promise, line of verse] by which he brings back into present time the origins of his own person' (E 47/255). By challenging Freud as Lacan's precursor, showing how at crucial points it is Kierkegaard that mediates Lacan, my aim is to draw Lacan up into the ecclesiastical narrative, song, or verse that constitutes the liturgical drama of the Eucharist.

Trauma

Mediating psychoanalysis and theology is my central metaphor: *trauma*. Trauma implies a break, deriving from the Greek: τραύμα, to wound: 'he went up to him and bandaged his wounds [τραύμα]' (Luke 10.34). However, in the last two hundred years trauma has made the dramatic shift from the material to the psychical. The impetus lay in the received cases of 'railway spine', in which apparently uninjured and otherwise healthy railway accident victims manifested a variety of physical disorders such as neurasthenia (general fatigue or weakness), intestinal distress and insomnia, and conversion hysteria (partial paralysis).

Introduction

According to the psychologist John Erichsen, just as a magnet, when dropped, may display no obvious lesions yet nonetheless loose its magnetic property, so too the shock of a train accident might literally jar the spine in such a way as to knock the nervous force out of the person. Arguably it was Erichsen who paved the way for the modern understanding of trauma by linking physical shock to psychic distress. The French psychologist Jean Charcot would contend that while intense fright could induce nervous disorder, fear was induced through a moment of self-hypnosis and accordingly cured through hypnosis; nonetheless, this merely confirmed the positioning of trauma as psychical over physical, paving the way for the studies of Freud. Freud and Breuer's study of hysteria (1893–5) consolidated the link between psychological trauma and hysterical symptoms, while positing that 'at the bottom of every case of hysteria there are one or more occurrences of premature sexual experience' (SE 3:203); although Freud would later describe as traumatic 'any excitations from outside which are powerful enough to break through the protective shield' (SE 18:29).

But, as Kirby Farrell has argued, whether physical or neurological, the effects of trauma are also psycho-cultural because injury entails interpretation and hence trauma can serve as a trope, condensing the fears or hopes of individuals or nations. A case in point is the aforementioned 'railway spine'. The perceived technologies such as transport and the telegraph started to collapse time and space; while elsewhere the sheer architectural scale of technology, from boats to bridges, both thrilled and frightened the Victorian imaginations (Farrell, 1998, p. 8); it was as if England were being besieged by iron giants, and trauma provided a cultural trope to explore that brave new world. Likewise, I employ trauma as a cultural trope to explore the Eucharist.

People are not merely the passive precipitants of trauma, people *use* trauma because a sudden interruption can encourage change. Indeed, this is the basis of the psychoanalytic cure. Where someone is experiencing a post-traumatic disorder, the way forward is to re-traumatize the patient, to create a second

21

or 'double' wound (Caruth, 1996, pp. 3–7); unsettling the ground, because, as Farrell puts it:

> Trauma destabilises the ground of experience, and therefore it is always supercharged with significance and always profoundly equivocal in its interpretive possibilities. Like traditional religious-conversion experience, it can signify rebirth and promise transcendence, or it can open onto an abyss. (Farrell, 1998, p. 18)

Farrell's reference to religious conversion is telling in that it points to my central thesis: trauma is a powerful metaphor for what takes place in the Eucharist. It is traumatic because its central image is of a beaten and bleeding man strung up upon a cross, and it is traumatic because as the liturgy unfolds we are called to identify as the perpetrators of this violent death. But it is also traumatic because it invites the absolute Other – God – into our everyday proceedings, asking us to take what is most mundane – bread – and raising it to the level of the absolute; it is as if a sudden tear in the symbolic structure occurs and lets slip in the transcendence; and this radical breach or *caesura* destabilizes the ground of experience. Where we see ordinary bread, it is entrusted to us to eat *the* substantially changed body of Christ. And because this trauma destabilizes meaning, new possibilities are opened up, new futures for world-building. Hence one can begin to envisage liturgy as a social, participatory and therapeutic practice. At the same time, I argue that the psychoanalytic account of trauma is indebted to theological accounts of the Incarnation, historically mediated by Kierkegaard, through Heidegger, to Lacan. In this way I show how postmodern psychoanalysis is already a form of theology, and hence theology, a psychology.

Informing the move to liturgy is also a deeply theo-political motive. As Farrell points out: 'In the Vietnam War, officers sometimes ordered new soldiers to kill enemies who were then revealed to be innocent civilians, deliberately using traumatic guilt to promote bonding among the new men' (Farrell, 1998,

p. 22). Perhaps then we need the Eucharist as the Church's counter-trauma. Through the Mass, in particular the consecration of and splitting of the host, a community is engendered by re-enacting the trauma of Christ's sacrifice. Called to identify with the wounded Christ, expressed through the doctrine of transubstantiation, the trauma of the Mass invites and establishes the peaceable kingdom.

Indeed, I argue that only the Church's counter-trauma is able to hold good on Freud's desire to see psychoanalysis as a revolutionary practice. As Elizabeth Danto has argued, Freud was a modernist; a social reformer caught up in the fervour of post-war Europe, he envisaged a new kind of community based on free clinics. But Freud's vision never took root, curtailed instead by a raft of policies favouring private health care (Danto, 2005, p. 2).

If liturgy can be shown to overcome this modern split between the public and private, by relating to everyone primarily as a member of the enacted body of Christ rather than a self-seeking individual, then its counter-trauma does not simply become one means to return to Freud, but the *sine qua non* of real analysis.

Finally, by articulating the Mass in terms of trauma, I respond to Lacan's desire expressed in a personal letter to his brother Marc-François – a Benedictine monk – to intercede with papal authorities in the hope of gaining Catholic approval and thereby doing 'homage to our common Father' (Roudinesco, 1999, p. 205). According to Roudinesco:

> Lacan was not really renouncing atheism, but he knew that his way of reading Freud in the light of philosophy and from a non-biological point of view might attract a lot of Catholics, who didn't accept the 'materialistic' aspect of the master's own teaching. When they read Lacan they felt on familiar ground, that of a Christian evaluation of human personality. (Roudinesco, 1999, p. 205)

Of course, this merely begs the question, why would he want to attract the Catholics in the first place? His elder brother

Marc-François paints a different picture. A Benedictine monk, he describes Lacan as having had a 'very deep personal Christian culture' during his early studies, ensuring for example that his children were baptized (Roazen, 1996, p. 324). Moreover, he dedicated his doctoral thesis of 1932 to his brother with the words: 'To the Reverend Father Marc-François Lacan, Benedictine of the Congregation of France, my brother in religion' – a feature omitted by Roudinesco. And he would later describe the analyst as monk, a 'solitary being, who in past times ventured out into the desert' (Roazen, 1996, p. 328). If the surrealists were shocked by Lacan's dedication, the Lacanians were not. François Dolto, Lacan's closest ally during the 1950s, was a committed Catholic, as were the Jesuit Denis Vasse and François Roustang. Perhaps then this is the supreme case of extimacy: Lacan's unconscious desire, hidden in full view, in the front of his doctoral thesis. In other words, this dedication provides the hermeneutical key to his work, that it is a theology, and hence only by becoming theology proper, can it become psychoanalysis proper, that is, speak the truth of its desire.

Plan of the Book

The plan of the book is as follows. Chapter 1 is largely expository, outlining the development of postmodern psychoanalysis. I describe its roots in the linguistic turn, explaining the contribution that Ferdinand de Saussure, Roman Jakobson, and Lévi-Strauss made. In particular I focus on their assimilation by Jacques Lacan. I explore in some detail the development of his threefold order of the psyche, and their implications for clinical practice.

However, this is not merely a descriptive chapter. It is usual in appropriating Lacan to treat him as a postmodern philosopher of difference, a kind of psychoanalytic supplement to Derrida. Conversely, by contextualizing his work within a clinical setting I highlight the radical sense of agency and action in his work, which governs his psychoanalytic approach; what

Lacan calls 'the assumption of desire'. I use this sense of agency in the following chapters to bridge psychoanalytic and theological goals.

In Chapter 2 I explore the concept of repetition (receiving everything back in a different form). Repetition provides the rationale for the symptom (the return of the repressed); it also forms the basis of the psychoanalytic cure – the analysand must repeat themselves on the basis of a difference, that is, free from neurosis. I argue that Lacan's concept of repetition is expressly indebted to Kierkegaard, for whom repetition is principally a theological category. For example, the Christian receives himself back on the basis of a difference (Christ). However, Lacan misreads Kierkegaard. This has the effect of arbitrarily closing down the dialogue between theology and psychoanalysis. In attending to this point I show that psychoanalysis can invite God back into the clinic. Indeed, drawing on Henri de Lubac's work on typological readings of the Old Testament in the light of Christ (Christ's fulfilment of the Law repeats the Old Testament with a difference), I argue that all forms of repetition including psychoanalysis become an *imitatio Christi*. This chapter has strategic importance in providing the link to the following chapters in which I *repeat* psychoanalysis: I argue that liturgy amounts to a form of social-psychoanalysis, both continuous yet articulating the difference that is Christ.

Given the centrality of the linguistic turn to postmodern psychoanalysis, for theology to engage psychoanalysis it must likewise engage linguistics. The aim of Chapter 3 is to undertake the dialogue between theology, language and psychoanalysis. To do so I engage the work of the Danish theologian Søren Kierkegaard with the French psychoanalyst Jacques Lacan. I begin by showing the centrality of language to Kierkegaard that, with the exception of Steven Shakespeare's *Kierkegaard, Language and the Reality of God* (2001), has been much overlooked. For example, Milbank recognizes that *Johannes Climacus* is an important source of reflection on language, but comments that 'Kierkegaard says little elsewhere about language' (Milbank, 1998a, p. 150). Likewise, the prominent

Kierkegaard scholar C. Stephen Evans makes a single passing reference to Kierkegaard and language (1983, p. 56), and despite Mark C. Taylor's later fascination with linguistics in *Erring: A Postmodern Theology* (1984), there is little indication of its seeds in his Kierkegaardian scholarship.

I argue for the centrality of language in Kierkegaard's thought. I show how he anticipates the postmodern linguistic turn, in particular Lacan's, claiming for example that the subject is alienated by language. However, whereas for the postmodern psychologist the subject's complicity with language entails a resignation to anxiety and lack – a kind of postmodern melancholia – theology is able to turn that very anxiety into an opening towards transcendence and faith.

In Chapter 4 I explore Kierkegaard's theory of stages or spheres of existence: the aesthetic, ethical, and religious with reference to Lacan's map of the psyche. I challenge the traditional reading according to which the various stages he outlines be read in a chronological fashion akin to that of developmental psychology. I suggest instead they be read as so many case studies which challenge the reader to look inward, and consider the manifold motives that drive us and thus recognize the irrevocable split that sustains the subject. On this basis I present a reading of Kierkegaard's *Fear and Trembling* in which Abraham, the paradigm of the religious, executes a role similar to that of Antigone as understood by Lacan: both have a purgative or cathartic effect on the reader. To this extent I argue not only that Kierkegaard's work amounts to a form of analysis encouraging the assumption of desire, but that psychoanalytic transformation amounts to a parody of religious transformation. As a correlate, I show the central role humour plays in Kierkegaard's theory of the stages, as well as situating Lacan as a prime example of what Kierkegaard calls a humorist.

Chapter 5 strengthens the contention of the previous chapter – that analysis parodies religious transformation, albeit from a different perspective. I show how the terms Lacan uses to describe the goal of analysis in his early work – *full and empty speech* – are nascent in Kierkegaard's work, corresponding to his distinction between a subjective and objective reflection, a distinction which arises from his critique of a passionless and nominal Christianity. Mediating the two is Heidegger. Having consolidated the relation between their prospective goals, I then move on to explore their respective use of humour in procuring that end. By highlighting their affinity I show the merit of Kierkegaard's work for clinical practice. Finally, I show how Kierkegaard situates his practice in analogical terms to God's engagement with the world. This allows me to construe God as the 'arch-analyst'. Building on this I make the claim that analysis, repeated through Kierkegaard, becomes a form of analogical participation in God's creative work: a work of love in which, like God, the analyst establishes a realm of created independence to help the subject engage in the subjective appropriation of truth.

Chapter 6 focuses on the relevance of time to psychoanalysis: one must go back in time and change the past, repeating it on the basis of a difference. I suggest that ego-psychology paid scant attention to time; the subject is encouraged simply to live in the moment, thereby becoming a slave to his or her own impulses. On this basis analysis can do little more than advise the patient to follow his instinct. By contrast, I argue that postmodern psychoanalysis adopts an approach indebted to theological accounts of time, mediated via Heidegger. The importance of theological temporality is the constitutive role played by God's traumatic intervention in history in the figure of Christ. By showing the historical mediation of theology via Heidegger to psychoanalysis, I make the extraordinary claim that psychoanalysis parodies this intervention in the clinic; thus, it is only subsequent to the Incarnation that there can be psychoanalysis at all. Moreover, because that intervention is part of an eschatological trajectory, one can say that only after the Incarnation can there be a genuine non-ego-centred psychoanalysis that does not lead to resigned despair.

In Chapter 7 I extend the relation between theology and psychoanalysis to the Eucharist. I argue that the Eucharist, underlined by the doctrine of real presence, amounts to a form of analytic intervention; the intervention of the Word, which as the traumatic point, becomes constitutive of time and meaning. Liturgy thus provides the conditions for a social form of analysis. However, ultimately theology surpasses psychoanalysis because whereas postmodern psychoanalysis assigns the subject to a despairing lack, eucharistic devotion points the subject towards the divine plenitude of God's love. Indeed, I argue that because Christ's death was the death *of* death, life emerges as excessive to death, and hence liturgy exposes trauma and anxiety not simply as the result of a lack (for example a lack of meaning, a lack of life, and so on), but issuing from the excess of life.

I

Lacan and Postmodern Psychoanalysis

Introduction

The aim of this chapter is twofold: first, to present to the reader an introduction to postmodern psychoanalysis, treating its sources in the structuralism of Ferdinand Saussure (1857–1913), the structural anthropology of Claude Lévi-Strauss (b. 1908), and linguistics of Roman Jakobson (1896–1982); second, to provide a comprehensive introduction to the thought and practice of Lacanian psychoanalysis, the exemplary form of postmodern psychoanalysis.

In developing his work Lacan came up with a trinity to rival that of Freud: the imaginary, symbolic, and real, which approximate to the ego, the super ego, and id. Taken together, these three registers form the fundamental system around which his theoretical and practical work turns. Accordingly, I have divided this chapter into three principal sections corresponding to the three registers. In each case I show how the register historically emerged in Lacan's work, how it functions as a register, and how it contributed to the maturation of his work. I begin with the imaginary register, and how it constituted the break with a modernist approach to psychoanalysis.

The Imaginary and the Break with Ego-Psychology

The basis for Lacan's disagreement with the climate of psycho-analytic thought, and in particular the dominant school of ego-psychology, was Henry Wallon's simple experiment with a mirror. The experiment was designed to draw out the distinction between a human infant at six months and a chimpanzee of the same age. Placed in front of a mirror a chimpanzee's initial interest in his image will quickly diminish; by contrast the child jubilantly assumes the image as his own.

Lacan reasoned that this was because at six months an infant's vision is more developed than its motor skills; so while the child is visually able, its body remains uncoordinated, giving rise to an initial experience of fragmentation and dislocation. However, in the mirror image the child perceives the promise of unity and autonomy, the image uniformly obeying the movements of the infant. As Lacan says: 'the sight alone of the whole form of the human body gives the subject an imaginary mastery over his body, one which is premature in relation to a real mastery' (SI 79). And it is the child's identification with its image that marks the point of the historical emergence of subjectivity for that individual, the birth of the ego. Nonetheless, the ego remains an imaginary or narcissistic identification that the subject makes with a specular image; the ego is therefore an alienating structure – its promise of unity belies the fragmented nature of experience. The identification with the image thereby introduces a split [*Spaltung*] into the subject between the illusionary ego [*moi*] and the empirical experience of the self [*je*].

In *Seminar I* Lacan says: 'The mirror stage is not simply a moment in development. It also has an exemplary function' (SI 74). In other words the mirror stage is not merely part of the child's historical maturation; it represents a *synchronic* function, i.e. a permanent structural relation within subjectivity. As a synchronic function it accounts for one of the three registers or orders of the psyche: the *imaginary*. The imaginary order, like the mirror stage, is characterized by a dyadic relation which stands for unity and sameness, a mutual recognition conferred by a narcissistic relation. Hence relations are imaginary to the extent they are relations of the same, such as friends who dress similarly or desire the same object; the desires and actions of each one confirming the other in who he is.

The imaginary is at the root of frustration, aggression, and violence. Frustration and aggression arise because one can never live up to the image of one's self – we are not primarily whole but discordant. Violence arises because in constituting oneself on the basis of another, one inevitably brings oneself into conflict with another over the object of desire – both will desire the same thing – rivalry thereby transforms desire into violence.

Lacan's critique has not been universally accepted. David Macey argues that Lacan's critique of the ego simply served as a pretext to denounce the whole of American culture, and therefore has more to do with French anti-Americanism in the mid-1960s than the history of psychoanalysis (Macey, 1988, p. 111). For example, Lacan says:

The academic restoration of this 'autonomous ego' justified my view that a misunderstanding was involved in any attempt to strengthen the ego in a type of analysis that took as its criteria of 'success' a successful adaptation to society – a phenomenon of mental abdication that was bound up with the ageing of the psychoanalytic group in the diasporas of war, and the reduction of a distinguished practice to a label suitable to the 'American way of life'. (E 295/809)

However, ego-psychology was already under fire from American ego-psychologists like Erik Erikson. Erikson questioned the unproblematic status accorded to reality in ego-psychology, saying:

Bolstering, bantering, boisterousness, and other 'ego-inflating' behaviour is, of course, part of the American folkways . . . . Without it a therapeutic relationship in this country would remain outlandish and non-specific . . . however, is the systematic exploitation of the national practice . . . submerging their anxiety'. (Erikson, 1959, p. 47)

Macey also highlights Bruno Bettelheim's work *Surviving the Holocaust*. Here, Bettelheim, a survivor of Dachau, writes:

If the author [Bettelheim] should be asked to sum up in one sentence what, during all the time he spent in the camp, was his main problem, he would say: *to safeguard his ego in such a way that, if by any luck he regain liberty, he would be approximately the same person he was when deprived of liberty.* (Bettelheim, 1986, p. 74; Macey, 1988, p. 276)

But to accuse Lacan of wishing to expunge all sense of identity in his critique of the ego is to miss the point. After all, the imaginary remains part of the permanent structure within subjectivity providing for a minimal level of identity between terms, without which no meaningful exchange could take place. A person's name for example belongs to the register of the imaginary to the extent it remains the same throughout their life; in turn it attracts particular types of identification, for example, a name can signify class. Hence what is at stake is not the imaginary *per se*, but the point at which we are alienated from our desire through imaginary identifications, for example the point at which we fall back into repetitive types of behaviour.

The Symbolic

The role of the symbolic comes to the fore in Lacan's work with the Rome Report in 1954. The report shows how indebted Lacan was to Lévi-Strauss during this period, an influence which stretches not just to Lacan's theory of the symbolic but also to its application to Freudian psychoanalysis. Given his influence I shall begin by outlining Lévi-Strauss's central contribution.

Lévi-Strauss

Like Saussure, Lévi-Strauss held to a differential view of language: meaning was a product of a word's location within a system of differences rather than an inherent property of the concept itself. Lévi-Strauss employed this structural approach to reading society. What counted when studying rituals was not any biological reasoning but the cultural symbolic structures, the system of differences superimposed on nature and mediating social relations.

Lévi-Strauss was particularly interested in systems of kinship. By looking at the relational differences between elements in rites of kinship he argued that despite the diversity of rituals a singular motif was dominant: exchange. Kinship systems do not prohibit the incestuous biological impulse of man as Freud had claimed; rather, the prohibition obliges the mother, sister or daughter to be given to others. The prohibition of incest is 'the supreme rule of the gift' (Lévi-Strauss, 1969, p. 481):

> Marriage regulates the exchange of women by treating them as a sign. Furthermore, 'The prohibition of incest is . . . the fundamental step because of which, by which, but above all in which, the transition from nature to culture is accomplished'. (Lévi-Strauss, 1969, p. 24)

Lévi-Strauss is making three related points. First, culture is a system coterminous with language, a relational system of differences. Second, culture is imposed on nature mediating social relations. Third, the pivotal moment in the transition from nature to culture is the incest taboo that surrounds kinship rituals, which is really a rule obliging symbolic exchange. Put another way, the moment we partake in symbolic exchange is the moment we become cultured. Lévi-Strauss describes his methodological shift from what we perceive as the inherent meaning of rituals to their meaning from a structural viewpoint in terms of the shift from conscious to unconscious: 'Structural linguistics shifts from the study of *conscious* linguistic phenomena to the study of their *unconscious* infrastructure' (Lévi-Strauss, 1963, p. 33). In this way he equates the symbolic with the unconscious; it shapes us and determines patterns of behaviour that at a conscious level are variously described.

Of Lévi-Strauss Lacan writes: 'Isn't it striking that Lévi-Strauss – in suggesting the involvements in myths of language structures and of those social laws that regulate marriage ties and kinship – is already conquering the very terrain in which Freud situates the unconscious' (E 72/285). What Lacan discerns in Lévi-Strauss's work is that society is organized like a language at the level of its unconscious; and that the law that governs the subject's entry is the law Freud names in relation to the prohibition of incest: the Oedipal complex. In other words, the Oedipal complex is not a story that has its basis in biological impulses; the Oedipal complex tells a story about a subject's entrance into language.

This insight would serve as the motor for Lacan's studies over the next thirty years. During the 1950s two tasks presented themselves: first, to give a more detailed account of the laws of language or the workings of the symbolic with a view to its impact on subjectivity; second, to integrate the theory of the symbolic into the theory of the Freudian unconscious culminating in his claim, 'the unconscious is structured like a language' (SXI 203).

As always, the precedence for Lacan's claims would be creatively read back into Freud's work so that what appears as a radical revision maintains a curious fidelity to Freud's text. However, it was to Lévi-Strauss's influence, Saussure, that Lacan turned to theorize the precise workings of language and the unconscious.

Language and the unconscious: Saussure

Saussure challenged the accepted view that language is simply a mirror of thoughts or pre-existing ideas, arguing instead that a word's value is produced within a system of differences. In rethinking language Saussure began by breaking it down into its elementary unit, the sign (Figure 1).

The sign comprises the concept (the signified) and the acoustic sound or image (signifier), the phonetic representation or image of the concept. The ellipse represents the structural unity of the sign: what is above determines what is below. The bar represents the co-dependency of the signified and the

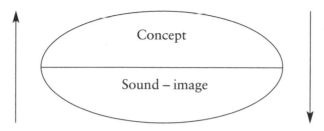

Figure 1. Source: Saussure, *Course in General Linguistics*, 1974, p. 66.

signifier. The concept (signified) and the phonetic sound or image (signifier) are joined like two sides of a sheet of paper.

Saussure's initial insight was that the signifier was arbitrary: there is no inevitable link between the signified and the signifier; the relation was simply one of convention and hence signifiers could change over time. But Saussure carries this further: it is not only the signifiers that change in this arbitrary relation, it is also the signified or concepts that change over time. In other words, the signified is as arbitrary as the signifier, so what counts as value is not some universal concept transcendentally secured, but the articulation of a sign within a system of differences: a word's value is a consequence of its relation to other words. In short, *'the linguistic sign is arbitrary'*.

Lacan fully endorsed the structural approach to language. However, he was not uncritical of Saussure's sign and accordingly introduces his own revisions (Figure 2):

$$\underline{S}$$

$$s$$

Figure 2. Source: Lacan, *Écrits* 155/515.

What are the implications of these revisions? First, Lacan reverses the established pattern of Saussure's sign. Instead of the signified (the concept) sitting above the signifier (the acoustic

35

sound or image), Lacan sits the signifier on top. The capitalization stresses the dominance of the signifier over the signified; thus, gone is the mutual dependence between the two. Instead we are given a hierarchy: the signifier itself determines the shape of the concept. In other words the signifier is like the sign above a door, and in the process of entering through the door the subject is capitulated to the signifier, given an identity within a system of differences.

Lacan challenges Saussure in this way because he believes Saussure's theory fails to 'jettison the illusion that the signifier serves [*répond à*] the function of representing the signified, or better, that the signifier has to justify [*répondre de*] its existence in terms of any signification whatsoever' (E 142/288). Put in different terms, Lacan's worry is that the sign still suggests that the function of language is to represent. By contrast the elevation of the signifier suggests that language is a 'closed order' [*ordre fermé*] (E 144/501), a differentiated totality that imposes order on life: 'We can take things no further along this path than to demonstrate that no signification can be sustained except by reference to another signification' (E 141/498). So instead of representing a thing, the signifier is the access, meaning is produced from difference alone. And language is characterized by the 'incessant sliding of the signified under the signifier' (E 145/502).

Second, to emphasize the dominance of the signifier Lacan abolishes the neat ellipse that encapsulates the sign (Figure 1). Gone too are the arrows suggesting mutual dependence. Third, the bar takes on a new meaning. For Saussure, the bar functioned like the arrows (Figure 1), as an expression of the co-dependence of the sign, the signifier and signified being as the two sides of a piece of paper. For Lacan the bar literally *bars* access to the signifier thereby 'separating the two levels' (E 141/497):

> One thing is certain: this access must not, in any case, carry any signification with it if the algorithm, S/s, with its bar is appropriate to it. For insofar as the algorithm itself is but a

pure function of the signifier, it can reveal only a signifying structure in this transfer. (E 144/501)

In summary, Lacan endorses a structural view of language yet radicalizes it, wiping out any last vestiges of the material world, anything that may anchor the subject in anything other than the system of signs that constitute language. Lacan's view tends toward a virtual world where at its most polemical even the question of sexual difference is not referred to the physical properties of one's body, but the sign under which one falls (E 143/499).

Language and the unconscious: Jakobson

As Roudinesco puts it, Lacan's operation 'needed more assistance than Saussure alone could supply' and he found it in the work of the Russian linguist and literary critic Roman Jakobson. In his influential paper 'Two aspects of language and two types of aphasic disturbances', Jakobson undertook a brief study of aphasic or speech disorder. Jakobson identified two types: similarity disorder and contiguity disorder.

In similarity disorder the patient can complete given sentences, but has trouble starting them: context is everything. The more statements are dependent upon a context the more the sufferer can cope. For example: 'The sentence "it rains" cannot be produced unless the utterer sees that it is actually raining.' Jakobson argued that in similarity disorder the patient suffers an inability of metaphor as a mode of function. He is unable to easily substitute words outside of the immediate context. In contrast, contiguity disorder 'diminishes the extent and variety of sentences. The syntactical rules organising words into higher units are lost; this loss, called *agrammatism*, causes the degeneration of the sentence into a mere "word heap" . . . . Word order becomes chaotic' (Jakobson, 1987, p. 106). For the sufferer of contiguity disorder, the function of metonym is alien; that is, he is unable to easily combine words within any given context. In the final part of his paper Jakobson suggested that 'competition between both devices, metonymic and metaphoric is manifest in . . . the structure of dreams' (Jakobson, 1987, p. 113). He links symbolism to metaphor (a relation of similarity), and condensation and displacement to metonym (a relation of contiguity).

Lacan reworks both Saussure and Jakobson's work into the unconscious process that constitutes dream-work as described by Freud (SE 4:277–338). In dream-work the latent or repressed content of the unconscious is made manifest (the process of *distortion*) through the twin themes on *condensation* and *displacement*. In condensation a single idea/image within a dream is used to represent an associative chain of ideas. For example, in 'Dream of the botanical monograph' the monograph condenses among others: his wife's favourite flowers, the forgotten flowers, his failure with cocaine treatment, and his neglect of botany (SE 4:169–73). In displacement, the cathexis associated with one idea is transferred onto another. In the case of Little Hans, fear of the father is transposed onto fear of horses (SE 10:90). Lacan suggests that the process of distortion correlates to the sliding of the signified under the signifier. Following Roman Jakobson, he then argues, albeit differently, that the themes of condensation and displacement depend upon the linguistic conventions of metonym and metaphor:

> *Entstellung*, translated as 'transposition' – which Freud shows to be the general precondition for the functioning of the dream – is what I designated earlier, with Saussure, as the sliding of the signified under the signifier, which is always happening (unconsciously let us note) in discourse.
>
> But the two aspects of the signifier's impact on the signified are also found here:
>
> *Verdichtung*, 'condensation', is the superimposed structure of the signifiers in which metaphor finds its field; its name, condensing in itself the word *Dichtung*, [poetry], shows the mechanism connaturality with poetry, to the extent that it envelops poetry's own properly traditional function.

Verschiebung or 'displacement' – this transfer of signification that metonymy displays is closer to the German term; it
is presented, right from its first appearance in Freud's work,
as the unconscious' best means by which to foil censorship.
(E 152/511)

For Jakobson both condensation and displacement are features
of metonym, while metaphor is linked to symbolism. Macey sees
the whole metaphor/metonym distinction as problematic. The
very difference between the results found by Jakobson and
Lacan should alert one to the fact that the typology is not as
obvious as it seems (Macey, 1988, pp. 162–3). One could also
draw on the work of Umberto Eco, who, in contrast to Lacan,
writes that from some perspectives 'metonym substitution is no
different from the process Freud called "displacement". And
just as condensation is involved with the process of displacement, so is metaphor involved' (Eco, 1984, p. 114). It is not my
task here to discern an exacting typography of the relations
involved, these comments should simply serve to alert the reader
to the complexity of the debate that Lacan's work overlooks. As
Macey sees it, 'the metaphor-metonymy opposition functions
adequately as a convenient – if schematic – topography of forms,
though . . . it can easily fall prey to the structuralist enthusiasm
for watertight binary systems' (Macey, 1988, p. 163).

Nonetheless, by invoking the twin figures of metaphor and
metonym, Lacan is able to theoretically underpin the unconscious with the structure of language. By reading linguistics
back into psychoanalysis, he brings out the forgotten flavour of
Freud's claim that the dream has the structure of a sentence:
'A dream is a picture puzzle of this sort [a rebus] and our
predecessors in the field of dream interpretation have made the
mistake of treating the rebus as a pictorial composition' (SE
4:278). All that remains is to rewrite the Oedipal complex as a
story which outlines the subject's entrance into the symbolic.[1]

---

1 Macey is highly critical of Lacan's linguistic endeavour. He argues
that it is a 'curiously truncated or incomplete version of the discipline'

The Oedipal complex

For Freud the Oedipal complex described the triangular economy of desire that exists between the child, the love of the mother, and the rivalry of the father (SE 4:262). The dyadic relation of the mother/child is broken by the imposition of the father, who triangulates the relation through a prohibition against incest.

For Lacan, the complex tells a more fundamental story about coming to be in language (SV 22.1.58). What is at stake is the Name-of-the-Father [*Nom-du-Père*]. In French the *Nom-du-Père* employs a pun because 'name' and 'no' are both pronounced '*nom*'. Therefore *Nom-du-Père* implies both the name of the actual father and the prohibition he represents. The 'No' is actually part of the mother's speech as in the case: *Wait until your father gets home!* It designates a limit, an authority

---

(Macey, 1988, p. 121). Missing from it is any attempt to provide a comprehensive discussion of other major theorists of language like Chomsky, Pierce, or Hjelmslev, while of the two he does discuss, Saussure and Jakobson, they are restricted to a theory of the sign and an analysis of aphasia. In turn, there is no sustained attempt to work through Freud systematically, exposing the linguistic elements that Lacan finds so pervading; and no account of or comparison with modern linguistics approaches. Indeed, the fact that most major introductions to modern linguistics relegate Lacan, if they mention him at all, to a few pages, suggests that 'his relationship with "modern linguistics" is at best one of marginality' (Macey, 1988, p. 124). Macey suggests that the only consistency is his inconsistency. Despite what purports to be a synchronic account of language, 'the discussion of Saussure and Jakobson coexist alongside a Heideggerean exploitation of the poetics of phenomenology and of the resources of wild etymologies' (Macey, 1988, p. 124) – although arguably this is precisely Lacan's strength. Macey continues: Lacan's use of etymology not only undermines his claims that meaning is synchronic, but also proves unreliable. For example, Lacan makes the connection between condensation (*Verdichtung*) and metaphor with poetry on the basis of the word *Dichtung*. In other words the relation is justified on the basis of etymology, which cannot in fact be supported. *Dichtung* derives from the Latin *dictare* and *Verdichtung* from the old German *dihan* (Macey, 1988, pp. 139–40, 280, n. 79).

beyond the mother that grounds her authority (E 208/579). As Lacan says: 'It is in the Name-of-the-Father [*Nom-du-Père*] that we must recognise the basis of the symbolic function which, since the dawn of historical time, has identified his person with the figure of the law' (E 66/278). And because the Name-of-the-Father is simply the support of the symbolic it is not necessary that the biological father serves this role, or indeed a man, it is only necessary that it is implemented. Because, without law, language and meaning descend into anarchy and psychosis.

Elizabeth Roudinesco has suggested a biographical origin to the term. When Sylvia Bataille, the then wife of the writer George Bataille, gave birth to Lacan's daughter Laurence, Lacan was still married to Maria-Louise Blondin (Malou). Because the child was born outside of *his* marriage, French law precluded the child adopting the name of her biological father – Lacan – so it was Sylvia's husband that gave his name to Lacan's child (Roudinesco, 1999, p. 163).

Desire and castration

In the imaginary stage, the child exists in a dyadic relation with the mother. In this pre-Oedipal stage the child strives to be the object of the mother's desire; yet properly speaking desire cannot have an object because desire is established through lack, lack in the symbolic. In other words, desire is a product of the differential structure of language. Desire arises because no single word can ever speak the totality of its meaning, there is always a remainder, and desire is precisely the desire to speak that which by definition cannot be spoken, the constitutive Other of language. For the child, the task to be the object of the mother's desire is therefore an impossible task. Lacan's name for the desire of the mother is the *imaginary phallus* – the child wants to be the imaginary phallus for the mother.

Entering the symbolic entails accepting the father's 'No', which signals the impossibility for the child of being the phallus for the mother. By ceding the task, the child accepts the constitutive lack in language. The child must thereby give up the imaginary dream of an attainable wholeness and allow a radical Otherness to sit at his heart, recognizing as a fact of law that the big Other mediates all social relations. The big Other is the governmental force that directs us yet remains spectral, never fully present to us; and in acceptance of the Other of language the child is castrated. In other words, castration is the inability of the child, regardless of sex, to be the phallus for the mother.

Symbolic determinism

In the Rome Report Lacan makes this comment upon Lévi-Strauss's thesis:

> In this structure, whose harmony or conflicts govern the restricted or generalised exchange discerned in it by ethnologists, the startled theoretician refinds the whole logic of combinations . . . . And this suggests that it is perhaps only our unawareness [*inconscience*] of their permanence that allows us to believe in freedom of choice. (E 65/276–7)

Lacan is startled to discover the degree to which the subject is literally subjugated to the role of the signifier. And this became his major thesis regarding the structural view of the subject, a point forcefully illustrated a few years later in 1956 with the publication of 'The seminar on the purloined letter'. Here, the circulation of a somewhat compromising letter to the Queen of France determines in advance the various positions the different characters play (the one who has the letter, the one who searches for the letter, etc.).

For Bruce Fink, being subjugated by the signifier has a curious effect on the status of meaning. Because the signified is always sliding under the signifier, the unconscious is that play of the signifier that appears in dreams, slips of the tongue, witticisms, or symptoms. The unconscious is always bursting through, threatening our lives with meaning. This is because the structure of the unconscious is the structure of language, which operates along the lines of metaphor and metonym. These figures, coupled with the incessant slippage of the signified, mean language creates a surplus of meaning to which we are subjected: meaning is not as indelibly tied up with the subject as one might imagine. Fink is not denying that our past has a meaningful effect on our present; what is at stake is the surplus of meaning produced by the associations our past generates. As Fink puts it, drawing on the example of Freud's case study of 'the Ratman':

> As a child Ratman identified with rats (*Ratten*) as biting creatures that are often treated cruelly by humans, he himself having been severely beaten by his father for having bitten his nurse. Certain ideas then became part of the 'rat complex' due to meaning: rats can spread disease such as syphilis, just like a man's penis. Hence rat = penis. But other ideas become grafted onto the rat complex due to the word *Ratten* itself, not its meaning: *Raten* means instalments, and leads to the equation of rats and florins; *Spielratte* means gambler, and the Rat Man's father, having incurred a debt gambling, becomes drawn into the rat complex. Freud refers to these links as 'verbal bridges' (SE 10:213); they have no meaning per se, deriving entirely from literal relations among words. Insofar as they give rise to symptomatic acts involving payment . . . it is the signifier itself that subjugates the rat man, not meaning. (Fink, 1995, p. 22)

Although we seek to make sense of the world, meaning is largely a product of the unconscious play of the signifier, curiously disembodied from the subject who, as a subject of the unconscious and language, is literally *subjected* to language.

Summary

The symbolic marks the second of the three orders that structure the subject. The symbolic stands for the realm of language, that is to say a differential system which operates according to the laws of metaphor and metonym; it is the realm of law, where the Oedipal conflict is staged and governs all social relations. While the imaginary is characterized by dyadic relations, the symbolic is marked by a triadic structure because it mediates all social relations and introduces the notion of radical alterity into those relations. Entering the symbolic entails giving up the unity offered by imaginary identifications for an all-encompassing structure that is devoid of any fixed relations, haunted by absences, and ultimately determines our decisions. For Lacan, the anxiety created by the symbolic, i.e. the *Other*, is at the heart of neurosis, and it is the analyst's job to help the neurotic extricate him or herself from the grip of the imaginary and accept that anxiety.

The Real

In Lacan's later work of the 1960s he became fascinated by the paradoxes that beset the subject of the symbolic and references to Saussure become scant. The overall effect of the signifier is described in terms of a splitting [*Spaltung*], a term Freud used to describe the ego of a patient which manifests in terms of two mutually exclusive psychical attitudes to the world. In *Seminar XI* this split is interpreted in terms of an impossible either/or choice (*vel*) between being or meaning that the subject must make upon entering the symbolic. The choice is impossible because if we choose being, the subject disappears and we fall into non-meaning; however, if we choose meaning, subjectivity survives but 'emerges in the field of the Other, to be in a large part of its field, eclipsed by the disappearance of being, induced by the very function of the signifier' (SXI 211). Hence one is condemned to appear in the division between being and meaning.

In his earlier work Lacan described this symbolic cut in terms of the split between the subject of the *statement* and the subject of the *enunciation* (E 287/800). The subject of the *statement* is the subject of the conscious dimension of speech, it 'designates the subject insofar as he is currently speaking' (E 287/800). This subject is differentiated from the empirical bearer of speech, the subject of *enunciation*, the subject of the unconscious, discerned only in terms of a 'shifter', a linguistic inflection that indexes but does not signify the subject. Lacan cites the French *ne* as an example (E 287/800), which, as Fink suggests, finds its equivalent in the English 'but' as in the sentence 'I will not deny *but* that it is a difficult thing'. 'But' introduces a 'hesitation, ambiguity, or uncertainty' into the sentence. The 'but' points to the split within the subject, giving voice to the subject beneath the surface of the statement without explicitly representing her (Fink, 1995, p. 39).

This is because as soon as we try to talk about ourselves we turn ourselves into an object. As Lacan says in 'Function and Field of Speech', 'I identify myself in language, but only by loosing myself in it as an object' (E 84/299–300). However, as Žižek highlights, this is not to suggest that the subject is some underlying 'interior richness of meaning which always exceeds its symbolic articulation', some underlying *ousia*. Rather, 'the surplus of signification masks a fundamental lack' (Žižek, 2002, p. 175). As Lacan says: 'I am not designating . . . the living substratum needed by this phenomenon of the subject, nor any sort of substance' (SXI 126); signification does not bar access to the subject, it masks the impossibility of the subject:

> One therefore does not speak to the subject. It [*ca/id*] speaks of him, and that is how he apprehends himself; this is all the more necessary in that, before he disappears, as subject beneath the signifier which he becomes, due to the simple fact that it addresses him, he is absolutely nothing . . . an effect of language, in that he is born of this original split, the subject translates a signifying synchrony into this primordial temporal pulsation that is the constitutive fading of his identification. (PU 265)

The economy of this paradox is summed up in Lacan's order of the real, the final aspect of Lacan's trinity. As Lacan says, 'what is refused in the symbolic order re-emerges in the real'

(SIII 13), hence the real is that which 'resists symbolisation absolutely' (SI 66). So when we identify ourselves in language, there is a negative portion we cede, the real. From the standpoint of the symbolic it does not exist, it slips out of view, hence its paradoxical status. The real has the status of the Kantian *'object in itself'* or *'noumenon'*, an object not discernible to sensible intuition, discernible only in terms of the effects it produces. It differs however in that it is not the transcendental support of the subject as it is for Kant, but the immanent inertia of the subject that evades symbolization.

It would however be wrong to simply construe the real in terms of a material substratum that refuses to be symbolized. Instead, the real should be construed in terms of the symbolic, in terms of language, because it only comes into effect through the process of symbolization. In other words, the real is not simply outside language, but the very heart around which language wraps itself: it is 'something strange to me, although it is at the heart of me' (SVII 71), the 'intimate exteriority' that Lacan calls 'extimacy' (SVII 139).

The Real Trauma

Freud linked the aetiology of neurosis to traumatic experiences repressed in the unconscious, and sought a cure through an emotional discharge, liberating oneself from the affected memory of the trauma. And just as Freud saw analysis as uniquely positioned to humanly deal with trauma, so too Lacan argues that 'no praxis is more orientated towards that which, at the heart of experience, is the kernel of the real, than psychoanalysis' (SXI 53). However, in contrast to Freud, for Lacan the real provides a structural account of trauma in the context of language; the *real* is the constitutive trauma upon which language is built and hence an antagonistic part of us all:

the encounter [with the real] in so far as it may be missed, in so far as it is essentially the missed encounter – first presented itself in the history of psychoanalysis in the form that was in itself already enough to arouse our attention, that of the trauma. (SXI 55)

The real is 'the essential object which isn't an object any longer, but this something faced with which all words cease and all categories fail, the object of anxiety *par excellence*' (SII 164).

Richard Boothby's elucidation of Freud and Lacan's comparative readings of the case of Emma offers an excellent means to grasp what is at stake in Lacan's reworking of Freudian trauma in terms of language and the real. In the case of Emma (SE 1:353–6), a woman has a phobia of entering shops alone. Initially she recalls an event whereupon entering a shop two female assistants laughed at her, upon which she quickly ran out. In connection with this she recalls they laughed at her clothes, and that one of them had aroused her sexually. However, later on she is able to recall two events some four years earlier when, while purchasing some candy, an old shop shopkeeper had grabbed her genitals through her clothes. In spite of this experience she returned a second time, but thereafter stayed away and reproached herself for returning (SE 1:353–6). Freud's question is, why did the second more innocent scene provoke anxiety, why the deferred action? He argues that:

> together with the shopkeeper, she remembered his grabbing through her clothes; but since then she had reached puberty. The memory aroused what it certainly was not able to be at the time, a *sexual release*, which was transformed into anxiety. With this anxiety she was afraid that the shop-assistants might repeat the assault, and she ran away. (SE 1:354)

For Lacan, what proves traumatic is not the physical assault as such, but Emma's failure to understand the desire of the Other. As Boothby puts it:

> What was he [the old shopkeeper] after? What did he want? The central point of the trauma was the question concerning the shopkeeper's desire. In this sense, there was something

unknown and unknowable in the original confrontation. It was an encounter with the real. (Boothby, 2001, p. 204)

In other words, the origin of this particular phobic reaction was not the anxiety of sexual desire, but our original dependence on language and the Other. In the encounter with the desire of the Other, the subject (Emma) was also forced to encounter the real of her own existence, the unassailable traumatic kernel of her being that resists integration into language.

Assumption of Desire

To summarize the thrust of Lacan's work thus far one could say: when we enter the world of language and symbols a gap opens up between the speaking being (the enunciator) and the language spoken (the enunciated). This gap generates desire, the desire to fill this fundamental gap. However, the structural gap renders the satiation of desire impossible; analysis therefore seeks not to satiate desire but to reconcile one to this perpetual state of non-fulfilment. Thus Lacan says: 'the symbol first manifests itself as the killing of the thing, and this death results in the endless perpetuation of the subject's desire' (E 101/319).

Accordingly one might summarize the ethical thrust of Lacan's work as an ethic of desire, where desire is interpreted primarily as a lack. The aim of analysis is to confront or revisit the constitutive lack upon which subjectivity is founded, to be fully submitted to the effects of the symbolic, to encounter the absolute difference upon which life is built, reconciled in some measure to the lack that is inherent in the symbolic and the human condition as the futile search for the lost object.

However, such a reading is, I argue, highly reductive to the extent it refuses the centrality given to agency in Lacan's work. For example, in his work *Ethics*, Lacan says: the only thing one can be guilty of is 'giving ground relative to one's desire' (SVII 321); and 'the ethics to which psychoanalysis leads us [is] the relation between action and desire' (SVII 313).

Let us set this in a clinical context with an example taken from a Lacanian case study offered by Marie-Hélène Brousse. A woman wants to have a baby, but she never finds herself in a relation conducive to her wish. She always ends up in abusive relationships. In analysis, it transpires that she can only remember her mother for one thing: saying 'I'm going to kill you', and in relationships she repeatedly assumed the position of someone scorned, someone disappearing, someone sitting at home making jam for no one to eat (Brousse, 1995, pp. 109–10).

Of course, on one level her mother's words conform to the object of her fantasy: death. Yet notice the context: the woman's desire is to have a child but, because she positions herself as vanishing, she cannot settle into a relationship conducive to that end, namely to bring forth life. In other words, she fails to assume her desire, the desire to have a baby. However, what is at stake here is not the desire for the object as such, but taking the risk of having a baby in the first place, which includes the acceptance of failure. Hence, seen from this perspective a Lacanian ethics does not mean reconciling her to lack, but allowing her to take the risk and find it in herself to initiate the act. For this reason, one should allow for the centrality of agency in Lacan's work.

Future Anterior: From Lacan to Heidegger

It is possible to trace this balance, between reconciliation to lack, and an emphasis on agency, back to Heidegger's existential phenomenology in *Being and Time*. Lacan's association with Heidegger has been well documented by Roudinesco. The two had met in 1955, and Heidegger had granted Lacan permission to translate his article 'Logos' into French for a psychoanalytic journal. However, when Heidegger was sent an inscribed copy of *Écrits* he wrote to the psychiatrist Medard Boss, saying, 'You too have no doubt received Lacan's large tome (*Écrits*). Personally I haven't so far been able to get anything at all out of this obviously outlandish text.' And in another letter he quips,

'It seems the psychiatrist needs a psychiatrist' (Roudinesco, 1999, p. 231). Lacan would later attempt to dismiss Heidegger's influence on his work, saying: 'for a time at least, I was thought to be obsessed with some kind of philosophy of language, even a Heideggerian one, whereas only a *propaedeutic* reference was involved' (SXI 18). However, one should not miss the mediating role played by Heidegger's favourite grammatical tense – the future anterior – in Lacan's early work.

In grammatical terms the future anterior is a compound tense comprising an auxiliary verb and past participle (the adjectival form of the verb in the past tense). In the future anterior there is always a future expectation, an act which is futurally disposed. For example, *I will be rested if I sleep now*. The past participle (rested) is conditional upon the present possibility (sleep). And because the past is dependent upon a future contingency, it may be retroactively changed or re-transcribed by the future. For example, *If I fail to sleep, I will not be rested*, i.e. the present is dependent upon a future action.

For Heidegger the future anterior is favoured as an expression of 'care' because futural anticipation and retroactivity are *temporal modes of the historicity of the subject*. According to Heidegger we should not be bored, day-dreaming, abstracted from daily life, but exercise an attitude of care which is to say one must 'use time'. In engaging time, Heidegger rejects the view that time is a series of 'nows' (Heidegger, 1962, p. 474), part of a great chain that trails back into the forgotten past while stretching forward into the great unknown. Rather, time is an existential category in which the past and future meet in the possibilities and decisions we embrace in the present. The past refers to the way we are already in the world, the way prior events or tradition have shaped, determined, or opened up possibilities for us. But our past also gets meaning from our future because it is redefined as new events retroactively cast light on what went before. The future illuminates the past in different ways that can coterminously affect the present anew, so the actuality of what has been depends upon the possibilities of what we do with it. For example, if my father was a carpenter, it is from my past that the possibility of becoming a carpenter arises, yet the past is only realized to the extent that I project the idea of being a carpenter forward into my future, which in turn is only manifest through *an embodied decision or act in the present.*

Crucially for Heidegger, an attitude of care is sparked by an encounter with one's mortality, a traumatic encounter with death. Faced with the anxiety, life starts to matter in new ways. Temporal nature impresses upon the subject the need to '*anticipate*' being with more concern (Heidegger, 1962, p. 387). The subject experiences himself in terms of possibilities and openness to the contingency of the future, but also 'resoluteness'. Through resolute engagement with oneself, being brings forth its own-most 'potentiality-for-Being' (Heidegger, 1962, pp. 267–301), and the past is reaffirmed in alternative ways, dependent upon how the future is anticipated. Heidegger calls the point we first encounter this new perspective the '*moment of vision*' (Heidegger, 1962, p. 387). The *moment of vision* occurs when the present is held in 'authentic temporality' and one realizes what it is to be concerned to the utmost with our being in the midst of time.

When Lacan turns to the goals of analysis in the 'Rome Discourse' he clearly relates Heidegger's use of the future anterior to *anamnesis,* the process of remembering one's past:

> what is realised in my history is neither the past definite as what was, since it is no more, or even the present perfect as what has been in what I am, but the future anterior as what I will have been [*gewesend*], given what I am in the process of becoming. (E 84/300)

By stressing the future anterior Lacan makes the point that the subject is always in a process of becoming or unfolding, he is never a pure event (E 84/300). But in the moment of unfolding, the future anterior also implies a moment of resolution, because the retroactive nature of being calls one to make a decision about *which* past the present will return to in the future, and its manifestation in embodied action:

[I]n psychoanalytic anamnesis, what is at stake is not reality, but truth, because the effect of full speech is to *reorder past contingencies by conferring on them the sense of necessities to come*, such as they are constituted by the scant freedom through which the subject makes them present. (E 48/256; italics mine)

End of Session: Punctuation and Interpretation

This sense of agency also underlies Lacan's controversial 'end of the session', one of Lacan's principal tools in analysis. The medium of psychoanalysis is speech, in particular 'free-association', in which the patient speaks without censor. It is the analyst's task to listen. The assumption is that speech 'conveys what it does not say' (E 81/294–5). People can say one thing while meaning another. Interpretation involves listening to the analysand. The dialectical nature of the analytic situation provides the arena of conflict where 'the sender receives his own message back from the receiver in an inverted form' (E 83/298) so the sender can hear what it is he or she is saying. This is achieved by punctuation [*ponctuation*] in which the analyst actively intervenes, repeating a word or a phrase or alternatively by leaving a silence at the end of the analysand's speech. Through punctuation the initial meaning of a sentence is retroactively reconfigured. For example, the accent in the sentence 'I am a child like father' may fall on the speaker's father: 'I am a child, like father'; or upon the speaker: 'I am a childlike father' (Lee, 1990, p. 89). By repeating a given phrase yet changing the punctuation, the analysand is encouraged to hear the subtext of his own speech, that is, the unconscious.

According to the guidelines of the IPA (International Psychoanalytical Association), the analytic hour should be of a fixed duration: fifty minutes. Such regularity ensures a secure holding space in the manner of the controlling ego. However, during the course of a session Lacan would often end abruptly. This unorthodox break in practice would eventually lead to his expulsion from the SPP (Société Psychanalytique de Paris) and later the SFP (Société Français de Psychanalyse) although as Mario L. Beira notes, not all those expelled with Lacan broke this rule; moreover, in Freud's case study of the Wolf-man (SE 17), Freud himself had experimented with the duration of sessions (Beira, 2000, p. 187).

Lacan's argument for doing so was threefold. First, the end of a session should be sensitive to the analysand's discourse. If the analysand reaches an important realization or stumbles upon something significant, with or without realizing it, ending the session on that point will highlight its importance. The ending can thereby serve to throw the analysand back onto his speech because he will inevitably ask 'Why did the session end there, what was the significance of my speech?' Second, Lacan argued that the analysand will imbue every detail of analysis with meaning and hence 'the ending of the session cannot but be experienced by the subject as a punctuation of his progress' (E 96/313). That is to say, even when the end of the session occurs due to pre-ordained standards, the analysand still imbues the end with significance. This being the case, Lacan argues that it makes sense to utilize this end to its full effect. Third, and crucially, ending the session bears on what Lacan calls the *'moment of concluding'* (E 48/257):

> the ending of the session – which current technique makes into an interruption that is determined purely by the clock and, as such takes no account of the thread of the subject's discourse – plays the part of a scansion which has the full value of an intervention by the analyst that is designed to precipitate concluding moments. Thus we must free the ending from its routine framework and employ it for all the useful aims of analytic technique. (E 44/252)

When he first introduces the term, it is one of three terms that collectively provide a temporal framework within which Lacan situates the unconscious. Lacan introduces this framework to give a descriptive alternative to Freud's belief in the 'timelessness' (SE 12:108) of the unconscious (Éc 197–213). Lacan begins with an analogy: a prison governor wishes to release one of three prisoners without taking the responsibility for deciding which one. As such he devises a plan. He takes five disks, three white and two black, and tells the prisoners he will place one of the disks on their backs. Based simply on the colours of the other two, the prisoners must deduce the colour of their own disk. The first to do so is released. The story portrays a time sequence within which the prisoners are situated: the instance of the glance, a time for comprehending, and a moment of concluding. The unconscious is situated between the instance of the glance and the moment of concluding in a somewhat elusive moment of apprehension. However, in terms of the end of the session Lacan's point is that freedom depends upon the quickening of time in regard to the moment of concluding: intervention 'annuls the *times for understanding* in favour of the *moments of concluding* which precipitates the subject's mediation toward deciding the meaning to be attached to the early event' (E 48/257). That is to say, the analysand is situated between knowing he has an opportunity to overcome his neurosis and bringing his neurosis to conclusion through an act of full speech. Interventions like suspending the session force the decisive event in the analysand. As Dany Nobus says:

> To put Lacan's principle in more psychological terms: through her interpretations, including the suspension of the session, the analyst has to facilitate and accelerate decision-making processes in the analysand; she has to urge the analysand to make decisions about his life in line with desire, despite the fact that he does not master all the knowledge necessary to be sure that the decisions are right. (Nobus, 2000, p. 159)

The end of the session acts as a form of trauma, an interruption that impresses upon the analysand the need to decide how he or she will re-present his or her experience and assume agency.

Conclusion

In this chapter I have tried to orientate the reader toward Lacanian psychoanalysis, its theory and its practice, with reference to the imaginary, symbolic, and real. For Lacan these registers are all important, assuming the status of transcendental categories. As he says in *Seminar I*, 'Without these three systems to guide ourselves by, it would be impossible to understand anything of the Freudian technique and experience' (SI 73). In the following chapters these terms will be put into concrete examples through the engagement with theology. In my exposition I have also highlighted the place given to *agency* as an aspect of Lacanian practice – often lost by postmodern commentators. This has important implications as my argument develops, because the role of agency in analysis helps me make the crucial link between postmodern therapy and the role of Eucharist. As I argue, one way to explain the Eucharist is as a traumatic event (the real) which stimulates the assumption of desire. However, before I arrive there, I want to explore the concept of repetition (receiving everything back in a different form) as this constitutes my methodological appropriation of Lacan as well as mediating the relation between Lacan and Kierkegaard.

2

Repetition

Introduction

Given my aim to 'repeat' Lacan in the Kierkegaardian sense of the word, i.e. to repeat the difference, this chapter is dedicated to this central Kierkegaardian category for which the highest expression is atonement.[1] As I argue, repetition is not merely a useful metaphor for the analytic process, but rather, the analytic process is itself already a secularized version *of* repetition.

By reconfiguring Lacan through Kierkegaard's theology in this way – challenging Freud as Lacan's precursor, and showing how at crucial points it is Kierkegaard that mediates Lacan – I draw Lacan up into theology. The resulting Lacan will be 'true' inasmuch as I maintain his central tenets, yet transfigured (repeated), taken up in the Name-of-the-Father.

By way of both an example and a prelude to the following chapters, I treat the very concept of repetition as it appears in

---

1 This chapter is indebted to previous scholarship on repetition. For Caputo, Kierkegaardian repetition constitutes the first project to 'overcome metaphysics', the precursor to Heidegger, and the first concept to question the 'metaphysics of presence', the precursor to Derrida (Caputo, 1987, pp. 11–36). George Stack emphasizes the ethical dimension to repetition as a task of freedom in which the subject chooses to develop ethically and religiously (Stack, 1977, pp. 134–7). Louis Mackey provides a comprehensive outline of *Repetition*, in particular the structural interplay of opposites within the text, taking in deconstruction and feminist issues along the way (Mackey, 1984, pp. 80–115). Mark C. Taylor argues that 'Repetition is one of Kierkegaard's most troublesome categories'. He interprets it principally in terms of winning one's self back through atonement (Taylor, 1975, p. 329).

Lacan's work. I show how Kierkegaard's use precedes and informs Lacan, but also how Lacan misreads Kierkegaard. This has the effect of arbitrarily closing down the dialogue between theology and psychoanalysis. In attending to this point I pave the way for a mutual dialogue, inviting God back into the clinic.

Kierkegaard and Repetition

Kierkegaard's concept of repetition arises in the context of self-development and responds to the dilemma of selfhood: how does one reconcile the contingent and changing self with its own sense of apparent unity through time? As Kierkegaard says, in Greek terms this is 'the relation between the Eleatics and Heraclitus' (R 148).

This problem had been central for the Greeks. For Plato, self-governance and development involved choosing actions that were good, but to avoid relativism one must know what 'good' is apart from its particular manifestations. For this reason Plato introduced the doctrine of recollection (Plato, 1981, p. 104): the soul is immortal, over the course of its life it has traversed the cosmos and hence knows all the virtues. Therefore self-development involves recollection; finding out what one already knows. In the doctrine of recollection the changing self is anchored in the eternal virtues which can be immanently recollected.

Kierkegaard's contention with recollection is twofold. First, it amounts to an avoidance of time: in recollection one sneaks back out of life into the eternal. Recollection therefore refuses to acknowledge temporality as an essential constitutive of being. Second, Kierkegaard contests any immanent anchoring of the self in recollected truth due to sin. Sin introduces a break between God and man and so the truth is obscured. The Christian thereafter must rely on revelation, that is, the Incarnation, to reveal the truth. To intuit the truth within is a pagan idea.

How then does repetition solve the problem of the contingent yet enduring sense of selfhood? In Kierkegaard's book *Repetition*, the pseudonymous author Constantin Constantius undertakes an experiment to see whether repetition is possible by trying to repeat a previous holiday he had experienced in Berlin. Unfortunately he finds himself thwarted at every turn. For example, he is unable to secure the same seats he had before in the theatre, and later on, he is disappointed by the same company previously held. His initial conclusion is that repetition is impossible. However, in a sudden shift of perception Constantius is able to radicalize this conclusion: 'the only repetition was the impossibility of repetition' (R 170). In other words, one can maintain identity in terms of *difference* rather than the same. So, to take Constantius' example, while one cannot go backward or forward in time and relive a holiday experience verbatim, that is, seek identity in the same, one can repeat the holiday by having an entirely different holiday but which nonetheless recreates the initial difference the first holiday made, that is, one establishes continuity in terms of difference.

Remarkably, in *Johannes Climacus*, written the year before *Repetition*, Kierkegaard had already situated the problematic of repetition in language.[2] The moment we inscribe or re-inscribe a thought in language something is changed, a meaning is altered and a 'contradiction' enters in, 'for that which is, is also in another mode' (JC 171); that is, even the sign is unable to maintain self-identity. However, Climacus also recognized that without repetition there could be no meaning because 'only a repetition of what has been before is conceivable' (JC 171). In other words, only through the act of repetition can words and meanings establish convention and thereby become familiar. The paradox not to be missed here is that repetition is the very thing which undermines meaning, yet without repetition there cannot be meaning.

---

2 Although not dated by Kierkegaard, T. H. Croxall argues convincingly that it was written in 1842, January to April (Kierkegaard, 1958a, p. 17).

This semiotic paradox is also expressed in *Repetition* by the young man who in a letter to Constantius writes, 'although I have read the book [*Job*] again and again, each word *remains new* to me' (R 205, italics mine). From the perspective of time, something cannot remain new, yet it does so because the reader never exhausts the meaning. The oxymoron *'remains new'* encapsulates the paradox of language with which repetition is concerned: repetition is the impossible condition of possibility. Repetition makes meaning possible, yet repetition is also that which renders meaning impossible because as life changes, things appear anew. A case in point is the word 'moot' as in a 'moot point', a point not worth discussing as it has no practical value; yet it derives from the Anglo-Saxon, and is a generic term for legislative bodies, groups that discussed matters of great importance. We can use the word because its repetition has established a pattern of meaningfulness, however through its repetition it has come to signify the very opposite of its early intent. Thus, far from implying sameness, the literal reoccurrence of some original event, repetition indicates the constitution of an identity through its repetition which will be something new, and even the inverse.

But repetition does not merely name a concept: 'Repetition not only *is* for contemplation, but . . . it is a task for freedom, . . . it signifies freedom itself, consciousness raised to the second power' (R 324, italics in original). Repetition is an existential task because it is through a decisive choice that the subject orientates himself, constituting his identity in a conscious manner. As Climacus says, 'Belief is not knowledge but an act of freedom, an expression of will. It believes the coming into existence and has annulled in itself the incertitude that corresponds to the nothingness of that which is not' (PF 83).

From the existential perspective, repetition involves a decisive change to the extent it repeats the possibility of the ideal self as an actuality; that is, it seeks to attain 'a goal that one had posited in terms of one's possibility of becoming a self' (Stack, 1977, p. 135). This movement is of religious/ethical purposefulness, a self-transcendence towards ethical possibilities. Hence in contrast to the 'backward' march of recollection, repetition is a 'forward' movement (R 131); it concerns actualizing possibility in the forward thrust of time. And because repetition looks ahead, it is related to hope. 'Hope is a beckoning fruit' (R 132) that stimulates the ethical and religious purposefulness of repetition.

Finally, repetition involves one in a choice which is not once and for all, but must of itself be continuously repeated. As George Stack's insightful commentary puts it: 'The goal of the movement for an 'existing individual' is to arrive at a decision, and to renew it in repetition. In a repeated decisiveness to become what one ought to be is found the continuity that is characteristic of ethical existence' (Stack, 1977, p. 135). And crucially, continuity is achieved because in actualizing a possibility, one brings together the tense achieving continuity of time; one projects a given potential in terms of future hope which is met in the present through an embodied act. Hence, as Arbaugh and Arbaugh put it: 'by choosing repetition a man securely unites his past and future selves to the present reality and unifies them into one durational person' (Arbaugh and Arbaugh, 1968, p. 96).

In sum, repetition co-joins the temporal with the stable, difference with agency, orientating the subject towards the historical task of becoming. Repetition does not step out of time into eternity; rather, it finds continuity in that most fragile and contingent of things: *time*.

Repetition as Atonement

Thus far I have explained repetition from the side of the subject. However, Kierkegaard tells us that the highest expression of repetition is the religious movement, the point where the subject wins himself back, or gains himself anew by passing from sin to atonement: 'freedom takes on a religious expression, by which repetition appears as atonement, which is repetition *sensu eminentiori* [in the highest sense]' (R 320). In *Repetition* the emblematic figure of religious repetition is Job. Job has every-thing taken away only to receive it all back from God, albeit in a different form (R 205). Notice that this repetition is figured by God: it is God who gives back to Job his family and livelihood. After all, if repetition was achieved purely on the merit of the individual then there would be nothing to distinguish it from recollection. Repetition involves receiving back what remains a gift by and of God.

This reliance on God is given its most forceful account in *Philosophical Fragments* where Kierkegaard's pseudonym Johannes Climacus undertakes a 'thought experiment' (PF 9–22). His starting-point is the doctrine of recollection. He begins with two observations concerning recollection: first, when the truth is considered in this way the role of the teacher is that of a midwife (PF 10), helping the subject discover what was already known within as opposed to teaching something new (PF 11); second, the moment that truth is acquired would fail to have any decisive significance because it would simply mark the return of the self which had otherwise been forgotten:

> The temporal point of departure is a nothing, because in the same moment I discover that I have known the truth from eternity, in the same instant that moment is hidden in the eternal, assimilated into it in such a way that I, so to speak, still cannot find it even if I were to look for it, because there is no Here and no There, but only an *ubique et nusquam* [every-where and nowhere]. (PF 13)

Prior to the moment the subject is simply in a state of ignorance and after, there is no enduring significance because in the moment it is recalled, it is also learnt that it was known from eternity. As Rae puts it, 'In respect of our learning the truth, it is not what happens in history that is decisive but what happens in our minds' (Rae, 1997, p. 7).

Next Climacus considers how things would be were they to be different. First, a gap must be posited between the knower and the truth; that is, the subject must assume to be in a state of untruth or '*sin*' (PF 15). Subsequently a teacher must bring the truth along with the condition. The Socratic teacher aids whereas, if the situation is to be different, what is called for is an utter transformation, for which no human is capable; and therefore the teacher must be God himself (PF 15). Because the subject makes the transition from being outside the truth to being inside, the 'moment such as this is unique' (PF 18). The moment is 'short and temporal . . . and yet it is decisive, and yet it is filled with the eternal' (PF 18). Furthermore, inasmuch as the subject moves from the position of untruth to truth, a change takes place, a 'conversion' (PF 18) or transformation that renders the person a new creature; the subject is reborn (PF 19). Subsequently the teacher becomes a '*Saviour*' (PF 17). As Climacus says in summary:

> Just as the person who by Socratic midwifery gave birth to himself and in so doing forgot everything else in the world and in a more profound sense owed no human being anything, so also the one who is born again owes no human being anything, but owes the divine teacher everything. (PF 19)

Richard Johnson is quick to point out that this thought experiment contains within it a thesis that could not have been invented by a human, and so while Kierkegaard argues that God cannot be proved, he inadvertently puts forward an argument (Johnson, 1999, p. 52). However, for our purposes here, the experiment illuminates our dependence on the God most aptly described by Christianity. For example: first, repetition requires a genuine change, which implies that the subject moves from the position of untruth (sin) to truth (conversion), rather than discovering what he or she already was. Second, repetition makes time a premium; history is the site that registers change and Christianity the tradition that recognizes the historical significance of time by advocating a saviour who enters it. Third, repetition relies on a saviour to illuminate and redeem us, without which repetition would become a form of recollection; and for this reason repetition is not only an existential task, it is the decisive Christian category, delineating Christianity from Greek/paganism. As Climacus says: 'The direct relation with God [recollection] is simply paganism, and only when the break has taken place, only then can there be a true God-relationship' (CUP 243–4).

Repeating Lacan and Kierkegaard

Returning to (or repeating) the question that opened this chapter: how does my project constitute a repetition in the Kierkegaardian sense of the word? First, I wish to repeat Lacan, that is to say, I do not intend to reiterate verbatim Lacan; rather, I shall present an account of Kierkegaard that repeats, albeit differently, the fundamental axis of Lacan's thought. In other words, I return to Lacan but only on the basis of reading Kierkegaard. Second, the repetition of Lacan is also the cotermi nous repetition of Kierkegaard, a rereading of Kierkegaard on the basis of Lacanian psychoanalysis. Hence, my aim is not to pathologize Kierkegaard, but to show how he anticipates Lacan's central theme, and in this way to argue for Lacan's return to Kierkegaard.

The retroactive reconfiguration of Lacan in the light of Kierkegaard is coterminous with the retroactive reconfiguration of psychoanalysis. By repeating Lacan I wish to establish a theological form of analysis, created not from an independent basis, but an atoning psychoanalysis. This repetition or reconfiguration of Lacan, as with all Kierkegaardian repetition, can be considered in Freudian terms as an exemplary case of *nachträglich* or deferred action. Freud used this term in connection with psychic temporality. Psychic life cannot be reduced to a causal and determining chain of events; rather, it has the power to retroactively change the past, revising the past in the light of constant development. For example, this is the structure of a symptom: the symptom sheds new light on a past event, illuminating meaning in different ways. Moreover, the symptom establishes continuity through its difference, so in the case of Little Hans we encounter a small boy's phobia of horses, which turns out to be rooted in his unconscious fear of the father (SE 10:42): *the symptom articulates the trauma through a difference*. And just as a symptom is structured through repetition, so is the cure. Through analysis one challenges past meaning with a view to releasing one for action in the present. Indeed, the goal of analysis is for the analysand to repeat himself on the basis of a difference, that is, to act in a manner that is not circumscribed by his neurosis or a particular pattern of behaviour.

Sarah Kay suggests that such a reconfiguration after an event [*nachträglich*] is the basis of Lacan's reading of Freud: Lacan's return to Freud is undertaken on the basis of reading Freud through structural linguistics, reconfiguring Freud on the basis of present understanding (Kay, 2003, pp. 18–19). This approach affords a Kierkegaardian form of non-identical repetition. What is at stake is not the return of the same, accompanied by the conscious recognition of this fact (what Nietzsche called the *eternal-return*); that would amount to the literal rearticulation of Freudian doctrine. Rather, by transposing Freud's work into the idiom of linguistics we encounter in Lacan the same radical reasoning that was initially encountered in Freud, an affirmation of what went before, yet an identity constituted on the basis of a difference.

In *The Fragile Absolute* Žižek points out that this structural paradox is the basis of the forgiveness of sin through conversion: 'Conversion is a temporal event which changes eternity itself' (Žižek, 2000a, p. 97). Through an act in time (repent--ance) one is able to undo the past and win back an eternity. Similarly, Lacan construes the effect of revelation in terms of '*l'après-coup*' (SXX 108).

I would add that this is also the basis for the Christian understanding of the relation between the Old Testament and the New Testament: the Old Testament is retroactively reconfigured by the presence of Christ. This interpretive approach is called *typology*. Typology is based upon the presupposition that

Christ fulfils the Old Law. Christ is the culminating point of a historical and sacred drama, and meditation upon the Old Testament reveals the way this drama is anticipated. Typology 'discerns in God's work of the Old Covenant prefigurations of what he accomplished in the fullness of time in the person of the incarnate Son' (Catechism, §128). In typology the relations flow from a prior recognition of a salvation history. The New Testament 'reshapes the meaning of the Old Testament' (Ferguson, 1986, p. 86), retroactively changing the way one reads the old scriptures and repeating the Old Testament (the letter) on the basis of the New Testament (spirit), thereby maintaining continuity through a difference. As Henri de Lubac points out, this makes typological exegesis no mere point of interest concerning early Christian exegesis. Rather, 'it touches upon the permanent foundation of Christian thought' (de Lubac, 1997, p. 6).

Typology is distinct from allegory in that the historical significance of the narrative is not overlooked in favour of a spiritual or eternal truth (Goppelt, 1982, pp. 42–58). In other words, allegory is not orientated towards the historical. By contrast typology sees events in the Old Testament as foreshadowing the New Testament. Typological interpretation is to be found in the works of the early apostles. For example, Paul interprets the Israelites' Red Sea crossing as a 'type' (τύποι) of baptism (1 Cor 10.1–6). Church fathers like Origen also favoured this method (Origen, 1979, pp. 189–91). However, the precedence is set by Christ, who refers to Jonah as a symbol of his resurrection (Matt. 12.40). As de Lubac writes: Jesus 'sublimates them [ancient biblical categories] and unifies them by making them converge upon himself' (de Lubac, 1997, p. 7). The Old Testament provides a context from which Jesus can speak, yet at the same time that context is transformed (repeated). Moreover, as Umberto Eco argues, because Christ was the first to reconfigure Scripture in this way, so every subsequent attempt becomes an *imitatio Christi* (Eco, 1984, p. 148). Thus one can argue that all forms of repetition are secular parodies of what was, in the first instance, a theological concept.

My attempt here is to reconfigure Lacan through Kierke-gaard's theology. By challenging Freud as Lacan's precursor, showing how at crucial points it is Kierkegaard that mediates Lacan, I draw Lacan up into theology. The resulting Lacan will be 'true' inasmuch as I maintain his central tenets, yet trans-figured, taken up in the Name-of-the-Father. Moreover, just as repetition is a decisive Christian concept/appropriation, so what follows is the theological work of the book, undertaking the christianization of Lacanian psychoanalysis through repeti-tion.

Lacan and Repetition

By way of both an example and a prelude to the next part, I want to *re-turn* briefly to Lacan's reworking of the Freudian repetition compulsion '*L'automatisme de repetition* [*Wieder-holungszwang*]' (Éc 43). The basis for Lacan's rereading of the repetition compulsion is language. Repetition compulsion refers to the way the subject is forced to repeat various positions or roles given in advance by the signifying chain; that is to say, the subject's position is preordained, determined by the route the signifier takes. This was the thesis of 'The Purloined Letter' although it was elegantly set out the year before in *Seminar II*:

> This discourse of the other is not the discourse of the abstract other, . . . it is the discourse of the circuit in which I am inte-grated. I am one of its links. It is the discourse of my father for instance, in so far as my father made mistakes which I am absolutely condemned to reproduce – that's what we call the *super-ego*. I am condemned to reproduce them because I am obliged to pick up again the discourse he bequeathed to me . . . because one can't stop the chain of discourse. (SII 89)

In *Seminar XI* Lacan returns to this account of repetition com-pulsion, and in engagement with Kierkegaard provides a con-temporary reading of the doctrine of hereditary sin: 'the inheritance of the father is that which Kierkegaard designates for us, namely his sin' (SXI 34). In Augustinian terms we sin because of original sin, inherited from Adam. For Lacan, we sin because we are condemned to do so by the concatenation of signifiers which are determinative of our behaviour.

Lacan unmistakably gives a novel and contemporary expression to the doctrine of hereditary sin; however, two issues must be raised here. First, this account of sin can only be attributed to the young Kierkegaard (1835) for whom a 'great earthquake occurred' (Kierkegaard, 1958b, p. 39). Kierkegaard had learnt of some news concerning his father which caused him subsequently to interpret his family misfortunes (Kierkegaard lost his mother and five of his brothers and sisters by the time he reached university) as a form of divine punishment: 'there must be a guilt upon the whole family' (Kierkegaard, 1958b, p. 39). The young Kierkegaard was therefore resigned to fatalism and despair and, encouraged by his Lutheran upbringing, felt destined to pay the price for his father's sins. By contrast, the later Kierkegaard adopts a very different attitude. When it comes to the question of why we sin, he chooses the language of psychology over the language of dogmatics to avoid precisely the determinative element of hereditary sin.[3] Hereditary sin undercuts the question of human responsibility by saying we sin because Adam sinned. The older Kierkegaard wants us to take responsibility for both our sin and our free will. How does the language of psychology help in this respect? Kierkegaard's starting-point is anxiety. Anxiety, he says, arises out of 'freedom's possibilities' (CA 155). Anxiety is a response to the limitless possibilities that are open to us in our freedom. In the task of becoming we can become anything, and the responsibility and choice are dizzying. As for sin, within that range of possibilities we can choose to sin or not. And if we choose to sin

---

3 Kierkegaard does not refute hereditary sin; his point is that to express belief in this doctrine is a way of identifying oneself as part of a community of sinners (affirming one's part in a language game) rather than consigning one to sin (Barret, 1985, p. 46).

it is not because we are ordained to, but simply because we can, because the choice is there. In other words a prohibition invites its own transgression for no other reason than the possibility itself. This is the meaning of Kierkegaard's enigmatic claim that anxiety is '*a sympathetic antipathy* and *an antipathetic sympathy*' (CA 42, italics in original).

Second, as Gillian Rose remarks, Lacan's account of sin resituates the subject in those determinative structures that Kierkegaard avoided (Rose, 1992, p. 46). I would add that this is all the more remarkable given that Lacan's work also contains a strong existential element. For example, the end of the session forces the '*moments de conclure* [moment of conclusion]', that is, a point at which the analysand takes responsibility for the way she or he interprets the signifiers upon which identity is hinged. Alternatively, one could cite Lacan's dictum concerning the ethics of analysis: 'Have you acted in conformity with the desire that is in you?' (SVII 314). Here, the outcome of analysis is construed in terms of the relation between action and desire. Perhaps Lacan, like Kierkegaard, found himself faced with an overbearing sense of determinism (in his case as a result of his meditations on language), and subsequently developed an existential bent as a corrective measure?

In *Seminar II* Lacan invokes Kierkegaard's distinction between repetition and recollection to provide a nuanced reading of Freud's concept of repetition (SII 87–9). Here, he builds on his remarks given in *Seminar I* where, in a truly remarkable move, Lacan relates Kierkegaard's distinction between recollection and repetition to Freud's distinction between the two classes of neurones: permeable neurones (Φ) and impermeable neurones (ψ). Permeable neurones (Φ) offer no resistance to the flow of energy through the neural network and retain none of that energy. In effect they act to simply provide a passage from external impulses to the internal network and are therefore associated with recollection (SE 1:299–300). Impermeable neurones (ψ) can be cathected with energy and hence account for memory. Impermeable neurones are changeable and hence associated with repetition (SE 1:304). In this way Lacan appears to find a biological basis for Kierkegaard's distinction (Éc 45; SI 100)!

What Lacan has in mind in *Seminar II*, is Freud's account of repetition from *Project for a Scientific Psychology* (1895). In this text Freud describes repetition in economic terms: repetition has its basis in the lack of identity that arises between a wish and the perception of the object that fulfils the wish. For example, suppose as Freud suggests, a child wishes for an image of the mother's breast that exposes the nipple. When the mind is in a wishful state there is a rise in tension and a discharge is sought in order to regain the sense of pleasure. The child's first perception turns out to be a side view of the breast only, the nipple being out from view. However, the child's memory dictates that a particular head movement brings about the sought-after image of the breast. Eventually the initial tension is dispelled in the identity of the wishful cathexis (the desire for the nipple) and the perceptual cathexis (the image of the nipple). Repetition is the labour by which the child goes back, retracing the neural networks in the attempt to bring about an identity of memory and perception (SE 1:329).

For Lacan it is possible to give this text one of two emphases: imaginary or symbolic, which correspond to Kierkegaard's distinction between recollection and repetition. One can either read Freud in terms of the imaginary (recollection) or the symbolic (repetition). With regard to recollection (the imaginary) the emphasis in the reading is placed on the identity of the wishful cathexis and the perceptual cathexis: the child's perception, in presuming the relation between the desire and the object constitutes a form of recollection. This is associated with the imaginary because like recollection it involves a dyadic relation of correspondence:

> Kierkegaard . . . discussed the difference between the Pagan world and the world of grace, which Christianity introduces. [In recollection] Something of the ability to recognise his natural object, so apparent in animals, is present in man. There is being captured by form, being seized by play, being

gripped by the mirage of life. That is what . . . Platonic thought refers itself to, and it isn't an accident that Plato places reminiscence at the centre of his entire theory of knowledge. The natural object, the harmonic correspondent of the living being, is recognisable because its outline has already been sketched. And for it to have been sketched, it must have already been within . . . Plato's entire theory of knowledge . . . is dyadic. (SVII 87)

With regard to repetition:

But for certain specific reasons, a change occurred. Sin is from then on present as the third term, and it is by no longer following the path of reminiscence, but rather in following that of repetition, that man finds his way . . . so you can see the meaning of man's need for repetition. It's all to do with the intrusion of the symbolic register. (SII 87–8)

The symbolic introduces a 'third term' into the dyad, the Other (sin), which disrupts the unity of imaginary relations. Thereafter repetition becomes the search for '*l'objet oncière-ment perdu* [the fundamental lost object]' (Éc 45). Thus, just as Constantius cannot repeat the past success of his holiday in Berlin, nor can the subject retrieve the lost object (SII 87). In this reading the emphasis is on repetition as the 'effort of labour' (SII 100) by which the child seeks an object, yet will never attain it because of the break introduced by sin or the Other.

Two points need to be raised here. First, for Kierkegaard repetition means precisely to receive everything back albeit in a different form, yet for Lacan repetition remains the search for the fundamental lost object, a backward movement that, as Rose points out, has more in common with recollection than repetition (Rose, 1992, pp. 102–3). For example, I have already suggested that Lacan's reading of Freud constitutes a repetition in the Kierkegaardian sense; one does not read Lacan as a sub-stitute for Freud, or to recapture the lost essence of Freud; one reads Lacan precisely to experience Freud as new. In this connection, Lacan's admonition to his students to read only the first half of Kierkegaard's *Repetition* (SII 87) takes on a great importance, because it is only in the second half of *Repetition* that repetition is reconfigured in theological terms as receiving everything back anew. Second, once repetition is associated with the symbolic, it is a short step to reducing it to '*L'auto-matisme de repetition*' and curtailing the creativity of repetition. Lacan seems to implicitly recognize this when he says, 'since this repetition is a symbolic repetition, the fact becomes established as a result that the order of the symbol can no longer be conceived as constituted by man, but rather as constituting him' (Éc 46).

In both cases of repetition (repetition compulsion and repetition), Lacan manages to stand Kierkegaard on his head. Where Kierkegaard makes repetition a creative opening to transcendence, Lacan closes it in on itself, making it a form of recollection and reintroducing determinism. In other words, Lacan manages to reintroduce the form of theological determinism that Kierkegaard tried so hard to refute. Yet at the same time Lacan provides a valuable psychoanalytic justification for Kierkegaard's distinction: Christian faith is predicated upon the acceptance of a loss associated with the symbolic.

Repetition and Religion

In this final section I want to suggest that the failings in Lacan's reading of Kierkegaard suggest failings in his critique of religion. For Lacan 'religion in all its forms' consists in various strategies to avoid the central void (*das Ding*) around which language is spun (SVII 130). In this sense he offers little advance on Freud's thesis that religion is a form of obsessive neurosis. Religion arises out of a need to defend ourselves against the anxiety of the real. The question I ask is how much of Lacan or Freud's critique of religion is dependent upon a refusal to acknowledge the existential or creative element to religion that is offered by Kierkegaard?

In 'Some Considerations on Repetition and Repetition Compulsion' Hans Loewald compares Freud's repetition compulsion with Kierkegaard's (Loewald, 1971, pp. 59–65). Loewald is quick to point out that Kierkegaard's repetition 'affirms the prototypical importance of the past, but here a prototype exists to be creatively transformed in the act of repetition' (Loewald, 1971, p. 64). Loewald draws similarities to the therapeutic process as a whole. He goes on to suggest that Freud's bias against religion may have arisen because he saw religion in terms of a repetition compulsion that ignored the creative transformation implied by Kierkegaard. Does not Lacan commit this same mistake? Lacan reduces the creative element in Kierkegaard to a compulsion to repeat which then allows him to make the claim in *Seminar VII* that religion is only ever a stopgap for anxiety, a form of neurosis for which Lacanian therapy is presumably the cure. Yet as we saw, for Kierkegaard anxiety was a creative element tied to freedom and responsibility in the light of possibility. Is this not also the aim of analysis?

By reaffirming Kierkegaard, showing how it is Kierkegaard's distinction between Christianity and paganism which precedes Lacan's distinction between the imaginary and symbolic, one can not only affirm Lacan, but also in that moment reinvite God back into the discourse, the lost object, to be rediscovered through the labour of repetition *and* as he who gives himself freely, thereby replacing resignation to loss with hopeful expectancy.

3

Postmodern Psychoanalysis
and Language

Introduction

The single defining feature of post-Freudian or postmodern psychoanalysis is the effect of language on subjectivity, and how that plays out in understanding unconscious desire and the direction of the cure. As Adam Phillips explains, whereas the enlightenment analyst knows what people need, the postmodern analyst knows that those needs are made of words; whereas the enlightenment analyst encourages self-doubt, the postmodern primacy of language leads analysts to doubt the self; and whereas the enlightenment analyst searches for wholeness, the postmodern analyst asks how we can bear our incompleteness (Phillips, 1995, pp. 1–17). To bring postmodern psychoanalysis into dialogue with theology one must therefore bring theology into dialogue with linguistics. The aim of this chapter is to undertake that dialogue. In doing so I engage the work of the Danish theologian Søren Kierkegaard with the French psychoanalyst Jacques Lacan.

It may strike the reader as somewhat strange to engage theology and linguistics by way of Kierkegaard.[1] After all, did he not

---

1 Several recent works have highlighted the importance of language underpinning Kierkegaard's thought. Hong and Hong write: 'Kierkegaard thoroughly analysed the problem of language' (JP 3:791). Arguably the most comprehensive treatment of Kierkegaard's view of language is provided by Steven Shakespeare. Drawing on a number of Kierkegaard's works he argues that Kierkegaard offers the resources to steer a middle

pour scorn and derision on those intellectuals and academics who would erect another artifice by which to grasp the essentials of reality? While there is some truth in this claim, by reducing Kierkegaard to an anti-intellectualist one misses not only his intellectual contribution, but the important source of reflection his work provides on language.

Indeed, as Steven Shakespeare argues in *Kierkegaard, Language, and the Problem of God* (2001), to which this chapter is indebted, the problem of language was central to Kierkegaard's project as a whole. One need only consider that if language were transparent in its operative power he would never have needed to employ his indirect method of communication – writing under the guise of pseudonyms from differing perspectives with a view to encouraging Christian existence. Hermann Cloeren has gone as far as suggesting that Kierkegaard's critique of Hegel was primarily motivated by concerns over language (Cloeren, 1985). Kierkegaard, it is argued, was deeply influenced by Hamann's critique of Kant. Hamann had rejected the idea that reason could be separated from sense experience to arrive at the pure forms of intuition. Such forms were not simply passive channels for the content of experience, but active forms of language because 'not only does the entire capacity to think rest upon language . . . but language is also *in the middle of the misunderstanding of reason with itself'* (Hamann, 1949–57, p. 286; italics mine). What Kant's transcendental philosophy 'meta-obscures' is precisely 'the sacrament of language' (Hamann, 1949–57, p. 289). This accords precisely with Kierkegaard's sentiment apropos Hegel: 'If it were the case that philosophers are presuppositionless, an account would still have to be made

---

path within the contemporary realism/non-realism debates (Shakespeare, 2001). Hermann Cloeren argues that Kierkegaard's critique of Hegel was a linguistic critique (Cloeren, 1985); Kresten Nordentoft argues for the centrality of linguistics to Kierkegaard's epistemology (Nordentoft, 1978, pp. 81–4, 331–6); Geoffrey Hale argues that the finitude of language was a nodal point that influenced his entire literary endeavour (Hale, 2002).

of language and its entire importance and relation for speculation' (JP 3:3281).

My argument then is simple. In the first half of the chapter I explore the relation between language and subjectivity in the works of Kierkegaard and his various pseudonyms. This will constitute the initial bulk of the chapter. Second, I compare Kierkegaard's account of language to Lacan's, arguing that Kierkegaard pre-empts Lacan's central insights. But this is no mere comparison. In bringing the two together I suggest that the issue at stake between theology and the linguistic model underpinning psychoanalysis is not the constant deferral of the sign versus a neurotic retreat into the certainty of the exalted father *à la* Lacan, but whether the symbolic castration which is the price of entry into language entails a resignation to lack or marks an opening to God's plenitude. Indeed, as I argue, the resulting fragmentation of identity through language need not imply the univocity of alienation, but the mark of a prior difference ordained by God, one which refuses an ego-psychology in favour of mediation and participation in and by others.[2] Moreover, because the anxiety created by language can be related to God's infinite difference, it can always be argued that only within a theological reality can anxiety properly manifest; however, from such a perspective anxiety ceases to be a category of despair, taking instead the form of grace by which we are specifically called to God.

Given Hegel's influence on Kierkegaard, I begin by exploring the former's thought on language before moving on to a more detailed appraisal of Kierkegaard and language.

Hegel and Language

The movement of Hegel's philosophy has been well rehearsed: one starts with the immediate positivity of a concept (e.g. being);

---

2 To this extent this chapter repeats the sentiments and is indebted to the arguments of Milbank (Milbank, 1993).

however, the failure to grasp the concept in its immediacy gives rise to self-relating negativity. For example, when thought tries to think the immediacy of being, being becomes so indeterminate it gives rise to nothing (in a similar fashion, when any concept becomes all-inclusive it loses all meaning). Finally, this self-sublating negativity restores the initial concept, only now in a higher unity where opposites coincide: being + nothing = becoming. This is the mould that language follows: 'Speech and work are outer expressions in which the individual no longer keeps and possesses himself within himself, but lets the inner get completely outside of him, leaving it to the mercy of something other than himself' (Hegel, 1977, p. 187). Speech is initially internal, arising from the thoughts within one's head, but through the act of speaking becomes external. Once externalized, language becomes alienating, degenerating into 'an external contingent expression whose *actual* aspect lacked any meaning of its own – a language whose sounds and sound-combinations are not the real thing itself, but are linked with it by sheer caprice' (Hegel, 1977, p. 188). However, in its external aspect it is able to help man to a higher unity in *Sittlichkeit*, the ethical unity of the state because language provides for 'ethical order, in *law* and *command*' (Hegel, 1977, p. 308), that is to say, through language we communicate, build bonds between each other and exercise law. However, language does not deliver us into the social state without remainder; rather, language affords us a higher unity, preserving both our individuality (the internal aspect of language, our thoughts and ideas, etc.), and our sociality (the external aspect of language, shared speech, etc.). Thus, according to Hegel, one can say that language is that which

> separates itself from itself, which as pure 'I' = 'I' becomes objective to itself, which in this objectivity equally preserves itself as *this* self . . . . It perceives itself just as it is perceived by others, and perceiving is just *existence which has become a self*. (Hegel, 1977, p. 395; italics in original)

Language initially alienates us by externalizing our inner thoughts, but gathers us together into a higher unity in the state maintaining us in both our particular and universal aspects.

Kierkegaard and Language

Ever the ambivalent son, Kierkegaard simultaneously accepts and rejects Hegel's approach to language. Kierkegaard's initial thoughts on the subject are to be found in his treatise 'The Immediate Erotic'. In an argument culminating in the claim that Mozart's *Don Giovanni* is best suited to express erotic desire, he contrasts music to speech. Echoing Hegel, he argues that 'In language the sensuous as medium is reduced to a mere instrument and is continually negated' (E/O 1:67); that is, for language to be understood one must negate its medium.[3] In Lacanian terms one could say that language is split between the enunciated content and its act of enunciation: if one focuses solely on the medium of a person's speech (the act of enunciation) one would hear only 'the flapping of his tongue' (E/O 1:67), the phonetic sounds and so forth, but not necessarily the meaning (the enunciated content). By contrast music is pure immediacy: the medium *is* the message. Yet despite this Hegelian sentiment Kierkegaard's work mocks the very possibility of language or indeed any concept attaining a higher unity. Thus, while music expresses desire without contradiction between form and content, the context of the opera refuses a Hegelian-styled higher unity because Don Giovanni's desire is indifferent to the women he seduces; desire is perfectly expressed, but unable to commit to the other as part of a mutual expression of love.

It is significant that this, the first essay in Kierkegaard's first pseudonymous work, takes the contradiction in language – the incommensurability between its inner and outer aspect – as

---

3 It could be argued that some forms of poetry rely not on negating the medium as sensuous but exploiting it, e.g. onomatopoeia.

paradigmatic for his critique of Hegel, because it will serve the foundation for a more general critique of subjectivity, itself refused a higher unity because of language.

Kierkegaard's account of language is given its clearest (if not longest) exposition in the unfinished and posthumously published *Johannes Climacus*. The work satirizes Descartes and Hegel's use of hyperbolic doubt for the groundwork of philosophy, a tool to purge thought of presuppositions prior to the constructive task. For Kierkegaard, in anticipation of Lacan, doubt is not merely the prelude to certainty, but indicative of consciousness itself; part of the existential groundswell of becoming: it is because there is doubt that we struggle to find truth, and the struggle gives rise to consciousness – not unlike Hegel's master/slave struggle for recognition.

By way of a thought-experiment Kierkegaard initially sets off in the opposite direction asking: What would the condition be for doubt to be non-existent? The answer: childlike immediacy.

> There is consciousness in the child, but this has doubt outside itself. How, then, is the child's consciousness qualified? It actually is not qualified at all, which can also be expressed by saying that it is immediate. *Immediacy* is precisely *indeterminateness.... Immediately, therefore, everything is true*, but this truth is untruth the very next moment, *for in immediacy everything is untrue.* (JC 167; italics in original)

Kierkegaard's point is that if one is simply a bundle of senses there cannot be cause for doubt; the question of truth simply does not arise; it is only when one starts to draw inferences from those sense impressions that the question of truth or untruth enters into the picture. This is graphically illustrated in *Philosophical Fragments* apropos Greek scepticism:

> The Greek sceptic did not deny that correctness of sensation and immediate cognition, but, said he, error has an utterly different basis – it comes from the conclusion I draw. If I can avoid drawing conclusions, I shall never be deceived. If, for

example, sensation shows me . . . a stick that looks broken in
the water although it is straight when taken out, sensation
has not deceived me, but I am deceived only when I conclude
something about that stick. (PF 82–3)

The question arises: What are the conditions that allow for
subjective interpretation? What is it that makes truth and
deception possible? How is the immediacy of sense experience
challenged?

By mediacy, which cancels immediacy by pre-supposing it.
What, then, is immediacy? It is reality itself. What is mediacy?
It is the *word*. How then does one cancel the other? By giving
expression to it. . . . Immediacy is reality; *language* is ideality;
consciousness is contradiction [*Modsigelse*]. The moment I
make a statement about reality, contradiction is present, for
what I say is ideality. (JC 167–8; italics mine)

Language cancels the immediacy of raw sensation because
language is an 'ideality'. That is to say, language uses universal
or ideal terms to talk about the particular; it employs categories
which do not necessarily exist. For example, if I choose to speak
about the particular chair I am sitting on, despite it being my
specific chair, I identify it in terms of the universal 'chair', the
same word you might use to describe the thing you are sitting
on (assuming you are not now sitting on my chair!). Thus
language cannot be identical with actuality or the immediacy of
experienced phenomena.

Nonetheless, language expresses the world 'by *pre*-supposing
it' (JC 167); that is, there is an empirical actuality or material
substratum that exists prior to expression. For instance: that a
particular wall in Berlin historically fell cannot be empirically
disputed, but the point is that, as Nordentoft puts it, one cannot
go behind language into the 'pre-symbolic cognition of the
surrounding world' (Nordentoft, 1978, p. 334). The centrality
of this thesis to Kierkegaard's entire corpus cannot be over-
estimated. In *The Sickness Unto Death* Anti-Climacus says,

'The concept establishes a position, but the comprehension of this is its very negation' (SUD 97); in *The Concept of Anxiety* Vigilius Haufniensis writes, 'the immediate is annulled at the very moment it is mentioned' (CA 10); in *Training in Christianity* Kierkegaard says, 'A sign is a negation of immediacy' (TC 124); and in his journals he argues:

> Actuality [*Virkeligheden*] cannot be conceptualised. Johannes Climacus has already shown this correctly and very simply. To conceptualise is to dissolve actuality into *possibility* – but then it is impossible to conceptualise it, because to conceptualise it is to transform it into possibility and therefore not to hold to it as actuality. (JP 1:1059)

It is precisely because language negates empirical reality that Kierkegaard accounts for doubt and its integrity to consciousness: 'Therefore, as soon as I bring reality [*realitœt*] into relation with an ideality, I have doubt. It is the same conversely – when I bring an ideality into relation with a reality' (JC 251). But more than that, it is this very contradiction between language and empirical reality that gives rise to consciousness. Consciousness results from the active attempt to navigate that contradiction: 'Consciousness . . . is the relation and thereby is interest . . . , perfectly and with pregnant double meaning expressed in the word "interest" (*interesse* [between being])' (JC 170). In other words, what constitutes consciousness or selfhood is the active role of relating ideality and actuality. Consciousness arises when comparisons are made between dissimilar things, when the given is no longer simply registered and hence 'consciousness is contradiction [*Modsigelse*]' (JC 168).

One could, as one generally does, take the relation of ideality to actuality for granted; that is, in a 'disinterested' way (JC 170), what Climacus calls a relation of 'reflection' (JC 169). In reflection there is simply the acknowledgement of the relation and hence 'reflection's categories are always *dichotomous*' (JC 169); language and reality are simply linked in a mutually confirming manner that Lacan, drawing on the mirror stage, will call an imaginary relation: one merely reflects the other. In reflection the entire problematic is simply overlooked. By contrast, consciousness arises when the contradiction between the givenness of things and their relation to language involves the subject in an interested way. It is not enough to register the contradiction (reflection), in consciousness the registering person himself is implicated: consciousness *is* interested to the degree it recognizes and takes account of the gap introduced by language. Thus, to the dichotomous categories of reflection – ideality and actuality – is added a third, *consciousness*.

> The categories of consciousness however are *trichotomous*, as language also demonstrates, for when I say, *I* am conscious of *this sensory impression*, I am expressing a triad. Consciousness is mind [*Aand*], and it is remarkable that when one is divided in the world of mind, there are three, never two. (JC 169; italics in original)

To say 'I' is to introduce the first division: ideality. To refer to sensory impressions is to introduce the second division: actuality. And to introduce the active relation between the two is to introduce the third division: consciousness.

In summary, two points should be made. First, consciousness or selfhood is not simply given in immediacy but arises out of the struggle between language and actuality. As Climacus tells us, consciousness is interest in the sense of '*interesse* [being between]' (JC 170), and also a participant in the struggle: consciousness *is* interest. In this sense *Johannes Climacus*' account of language can be said to underpin Anti-Climacus' celebrated account of the self in *The Sickness Unto Death*:

> A human being is a spirit. But what is spirit? Spirit is the self. But what is the self? The self is a relation that relates itself to itself or is the relation's relating itself to itself in the relation; the self is not the relation but is the relation's relating itself to itself. A human being is a synthesis of the infinite and the finite, of the temporal and the eternal, of freedom and neces-

sity, in short, a synthesis. A synthesis is a relation between two. Considered in this way, a human being is still not a self.

In the relation between two, the relation is the third as a negative unity, and the two relate to the relation and in the relation to the relation . . . . If, however, the relation relates itself to itself, this relation is the positive third term, and this is the self. (SUD 13)

The self is not simply *the* relation of the contradiction between eternal/temporal or possibility/necessity; such a relation would be a relation of reflection. Rather, as the last line suggests, self-hood arises only in the act of *positively relating* the two as a negative unity.

Second, consciousness does not emerge as a higher unity in which all doubt is expelled. Language and actuality are a contradiction and so there can be no surmounting that fact. Actuality and ideality do not merge into a kind of cosmic 'One' which we call consciousness; rather, as Shakespeare puts it in his commentary on *Johannes Climacus*, 'Consciousness is doubled from the start for it always presupposes something which makes it possible [actuality], but which it cannot grasp in any straightforward way' (Shakespeare, 2001, p. 60). Describing the implication for consciousness he adds:

the collision between the real and the ideal, the singular and the universal becomes actual and existential. Language exhibits and embodies this transition and collision. There is no primordial foundation of consciousness and language, in which the speaker is fully present to himself in his utterance. As soon as I use language I am divided. (Shakespeare, 2001, p. 61)

As for that portion of actuality which exceeds ideality and manifests doubt, it should be noted that this becomes the motor of consciousness inasmuch as it generates the interest, becoming the impetus for the existential task. Doubt is a struggle that must be undertaken in every instance, rather than a malaise of the intellect to be overcome through rationalization. For this reason Arburgh and Arburgh suggest that doubt really takes the form of despair in *Johannes Climacus* (Arburgh and Arburgh, 1968, pp. 120–1): 'Doubt is thought's despair; despair is personality's doubt' (E/O 2:211); and despair, as we shall see, is not a category of privation or resignation, but of grace.

The centrality of language to Kierkegaard's corpus can equally be approached through the theme of fragmentation. Geoffrey Hale has argued for its conceptual pre-eminence in Kierkegaard's work. He cites its prominence in the titles such as *Philosophical Fragments, Either/Or: A Fragment of Life*, 'The tragic in ancient drama: a venture in fragmentary endeavour'; explicit writings on the theme within the authorship; and its implicit role in the assumption behind the pseudonymous authorship (Hale, 2002, pp. 13–15).

The most extended reflection on fragmentation is to be found in one of the letters that constitutes *Either/Or*: 'The tragic in ancient drama'. Here, the anonymous author, known simply as 'author A', provides a reflection on the motif of tragedy, and a comparison between its ancient and modern forms. Within this 'fragmentary endeavour' there is a short methodological aside, 'a fragment within a fragment' (Hale, 2002, p. 13), in which author A states:

> It is at variance with the aims of our association to provide coherent works or larger unities, since it is not our intention to labour on the Tower of Babel that God in his own righteousness can descend and destroy, since we are in consciousness that such confusion justly occurred, acknowledge as characteristic of all human endeavour in its truth that it is fragmentary, that it is precisely this which distinguishes it from nature's infinite coherence, that an individual's wealth consists specifically in his capacity for a fragmentary prodigality . . . . A completely finished work is disproportionate to the poetising personality; because of the disjointed and desultory character of unfinished papers, one feels a need to poeticise the personality along with them. . . . . The art, then,

is to produce skilfully the same effect, the same carelessness and fortuitousness, the same anacoluthic [*anakoluthisk*] thought process; the art is to evoke an enjoyment that is never present tense. (E/O 1:151–2)[4]

Kierkegaard links fragmentation to the biblical story of language. In doing so he provides theological grounding to his remarkable thesis that fragmentation is the basis of all human attempts to establish meaning. Yet such a thesis is not meant to consign the reader to relativity because first, the very claim itself situates one within an existing biblical tradition; second, fragmentation is deemed both the logical effect of language and a positive attribution ordained by God, a 'wealth' to equal 'nature's infinite coherence' such that every finite text (including the self) necessarily finds its *telos* in God. For this reason the author A prescribes for thought the term anacoluthic [*anakoluthisk*]: *a grammatical break or interruption*. Thinking should be self-fracturing, continuously curtailing its own coherence lest it slip into *sub specie aeterni*, while simultaneously referring the subject to that which is infinite coherence: God.

In this respect one should make reference to Kierkegaard's other allusion to Babel:

Perhaps the story of the Babylonian confusion of tongues may be explained in this way, that it was an attempt to construct an arbitrarily formed common language, which, since it lacked fully integrative commonality, necessarily broke up into the most disparate differences, for here it is a matter of the *totum est parte sua prius*, which was not understood. (JP 3:3281)

Notice that Kierkegaard does not read the story in terms of God's action disseminating an original adamic language.

---

4 Is this not the most succinct definition of *jouissance*? As Lacan says, '*jouissance* is prohibited [*interdite*] to whomever speaks' (E 306/821). Fragmentation alienates the subject and precludes any enjoyment being fully present.

Instead he reads the story in the light of Genesis 10.31–32, positing a prior fragmentation of language. From this perspective, God's act counsels against any arbitrary imposition of unity over the original dissemination – the ordained goodness of creation. Such an account accords with Lacan's interpretation of Freud's *Totem and Taboo*. Read from the perspective of *jouissance*, the prohibitions instigated in the wake of the primal murder, were *not* put in place to deny future access to the women. Rather, they hid the fact that there never was access to the female (SVII 176); the guilt of the group was such that they instigated the laws before the women could be enjoyed. Likewise, God's 'No' at Babel was not designed to supplant the unbounded *jouissance* of an adamic language (the pure mediation of God), it signals the fact there never was one; God's 'No' affirms a prior difference because God stands precisely *for* difference.

From this one can conclude: first, Kierkegaard's God is not invoked as a neurotic defence against difference, but is instead the very principle *of* difference. Second, this has a positive effect on how one views castration or the 'No' of the father. For Lacan, castration remains a necessary suppression, at once sparing us from the anxiety of not knowing precisely what we are for the mother, while asking us to accept that the signifier of wholeness will forever elude our grasp; it is but a figment as illusionary as the emperor's new clothes. Yet for Kierkegaard, the law enacted through God's 'No' affirms a prior difference. Thus while no less problematic apropos one's relation to law – we avoid God in the manner we avoid any challenge to our neat-narcissistic life that the Law entails – the embrace of law need not be construed as a resignation to lack, but the very opposite: we are entertained by the plenitude of God's difference.

Hale's own argument culminates in the claim that the fragmentary and finite nature of language is the basis for the pseudonymous authorship (Hale, 2002, p. 26). If all writing is fragmentary then meaning remains uncertain, and this extends to 'Kierkegaard himself, whose work is characterised not by a singularity of authority, but by the multiplicity of pseudonymous "authors"' (Hale, 2002, p. 15). As such, Kierkegaard's pseudonyms are less a trick employed by an authoritative author to seduce his readers into one or another belief; rather, they are already inherent in language itself. Indeed, Kierkegaard intimates as much in his journals:

> The difficulty in publishing anything about the authorship is and remains that, without my knowing it positively, I really have been used, and now for the first time I understand and comprehend the whole – but then I cannot, after all, say: *I*. At most I can say (that is, given my scrupulous demand for the truth): this is how I now understand the productivity of the past. . . . But this is my limitation – I am a pseudonym. (JP 6:6505)

Hale takes this to imply that:

> language and subjectivity remain irreconcilable, and this irreconcilability itself exceeds the delimitations of cognition. It cannot itself be known within language, because it is already the effect of language. Language produces the subject as its own excluded outside. To say 'I,' as in the sense Kierkegaard does in the journal, is to be used by language without knowing it. (Hale, 2002, p. 15)

Hale may have overstretched his argument here. Given the fragmentation of the text and authorship, Hale cautions against any 'categorical determination', such as 'theology', in guiding a reading of Kierkegaard's texts (Hale, 2002, p. 2). Where he confronts Kierkegaard's own claims for a religious purpose to the texts in *Points of View*, he says that these comments do 'little to clarify the "careless" and "desultory" quality of the work' (Hale, 2002, p. 24), and that Kierkegaard 'offers no revelation of a hitherto unacknowledged secret; it does not attempt in this way to correct an otherwise misled authorship' (p. 25). He goes on to add that 'even during this time when Kierkegaard was busily "orientating" his readers towards the singularly "religious" teleology . . . he continued to harbour doubts about the feasibility' (Hale, 2002, p. 27). Hale therefore concludes that despite accepting authorship, Kierkegaard stops short of being authoritative.

Hale may be consistent with Kierkegaard in assuming that our finitude precludes any God's-eye view of truth or authority: we cannot claim to be the harbinger of the definitive definition of Christianity, but this is not a licence for the wholesale refusal of any authority as Hale takes it to mean. What Hale manages to leave out is that Kierkegaard does not advocate the end of any authoritative voice, but the very opposite: absolute submission to God.

However, Hale clearly grasps Kierkegaard's point: language produces us at the expense of excluding us; and for this reason Kierkegaard is as much used as a user of language. In connection with, and by way of consolidation, one should return to author A's essay 'The immediate erotic' in *Either/Or*. The argument is that *Don Giovanni* is not only a classic, but the *greatest* of all classics. This raises an obvious contention: given that the author has defined a classic in terms of attaining a perfect balance of form and matter, is it not problematic to consider any one classic better than another since they are all defined by the same criteria? Yet author A seems unperturbed by such self-contradiction. Indeed, he suggests that such a self-contradiction is deeply rooted in human nature: 'Thought [is] continually going beyond itself and continually collapsing back into itself' (E/O 1:58). It would be tempting to consider this as an aesthetic problem, rooted in the particular character type of author A, yet in *The Concept of Anxiety* Kierkegaard's pseudonym Vigilius Haufniensis makes a similar point apropos language:

> If one were to say further that it then becomes a question of how the first man learnt to speak, I would answer . . . that the question lies beyond the scope of the present investigation. However, this must not be understood in the manner of

modern philosophy as though my reply were evasive, suggesting that I *could* answer the question in another place. (CA 47n.)

Simply put, one cannot think the beginning of language any more than one can think the absolute, because the nature of language is such that we are already always begun; our beginning lies elsewhere because we are split from within; yet one is compelled to ask these deeply problematic and unanswerable questions concerning origins, pushing thought beyond itself. And by prompting the unanswerable, language excludes that which it produces. Is this not the central dilemma for Kierkegaard: mediacy cancels immediacy?

Kierkegaard and Lacan

In the following sections I bring Kierkegaard into proximity with Lacan through a direct comparison of their linguistic doctrines. In this way I argue, not simply that Kierkegaard pre-empts Lacan's major thought on language and subjectivity, but that Lacan's approach has been actively promoted by theology. In this way I am able to subvert Lacan's atheism. God cannot be reduced to a stopgap against the anxiety of the real, any more than Christianity can be reduced to a social form of neurosis. On the contrary, to be a Christian is to be truly anxious because Christ is the most ambiguous of *all* signs and the stakes the highest: eternity. Therefore if psychoanalysis is to take anxiety seriously, it must begin by taking theology seriously. My argument is formulated in seven points.

The initial point of contact between Kierkegaard and Lacan's linguistic thought is that language and empirical reality are mutually exclusive. Kierkegaard expresses this in terms of language annulling actuality: 'A sign is a negation of immediacy' (TC 124). This directly corresponds to Lacan's claim: 'the symbol first manifests itself as the killing of the thing' (E 101/319); a sentiment later expressed through the distinction between the act of enunciation and enunciated content. Linking Kierkegaard and Lacan is of course Hegel, mediated to Lacan via Kojève: 'all *conceptual* understanding (*Begreifen*) is equivalent to a *murder*' (Kojève, 1969, p. 140).

Second, both consider the paradox between language and actuality as paradigmatic for subjectivity. For Lacan we identify ourselves in language, but only at the expense of losing our self in it as an object (E 84/299). The paradox of language – that it must negate the very thing it talks of, is the very structure of subjectivity itself. Likewise, Climacus says, 'The moment I make a statement contradiction is present, for what I say is ideality' (JC 168); using language introduces contradiction into the world because we only experience the world mediately.

Third, both consider language to effect an alienating objectification of the subject. Thus Kierkegaard refers to language as an 'ideality'; it treats us in ideal form, necessarily precluding the specificity of that to which it refers. Likewise, Lacan accuses language of turning us into an 'object' (E 84/299).

Fourth, Kierkegaard and Lacan both describe the experience of language as alienating. At this point we must define our term 'alienation' carefully. When Jacques Alain-Miller asked of Lacan '*Do you not wish to show, all the same, . . . the alienation of a subject who has received the definition of being born in, constituted by, and ordered in a field that is exterior to him?*' (SXI 215), Lacan answered 'very good' (SXI 215). That is to say, we are alienated because we are constituted in advance by the language we are born into. And this seems to be Kierkegaard's point when he complains of being 'used' (JP 6:6505) by language, adding: 'I cannot, after all, say: *I* . . . . But this is my limitation – I am a pseudonym' (JP 6:6505). As Hale says, commenting on this passage, what 'Kierkegaard demonstrates [. . .] is [that] it is not the subject who controls the communication, but rather the inverse' (Hale, 2002, p. 10); to use language is to be used by it; it is to be positioned by the very terms we seek to position. Hence while Kierkegaard manipulates his pseudonyms, he feels that he himself is no less a pseudonym, a fictitious creation. To put it in more explicitly Lacanian terms: the truth of our experience lies outside ourselves as opposed to being buried deep within us because 'our selves are somewhere else in the Symbolic formations which always precede us and in the Real which we have to disavow if we are to enter the Symbolic order'.[5]

In this regard one could also put forward a Lacanian account of the pseudonyms. In what amounts to a reversal of Josiah Thompson's thesis that the pseudonyms are experimental characters, suits so to speak, tried on by Kierkegaard to find a mode of existence that would overcome his loneliness (Thompson, 1967, p. 71), I suggest that Kierkegaard himself is simply an effect of the pseudonymous characters. When we try to identify Kierkegaard behind the pseudonymous texts we simply name what Lacan calls the *objet petit a*, the signifier of lack. That is to say, we posit the name 'Kierkegaard' to resolve our inability to fully account for the authorship or finally comprehend its whole; and although one could point to the direct communications, that is, the works signed by Kierkegaard, the point is that this is simply another pseudonymous character that happens to have the same name as the signifier we designate for the whole. This argument should be further supplemented with Žižek's perspective which takes into account the ideological gesture involved: any such attempt to say who Kierkegaard is remains ideological in the sense that it is an attempt to name the unnameable and thereby control the field of representation; and indeed, Hale's own work unwittingly acknowledges this when he says of Kierkegaard that he can only be a 'nothing' (Hale, 2002, p. 26).

The alienating effect of language can be further felt reading 'The immediate erotic' in conjunction with *Philosophical Fragments*. Both make the point that thought is 'continually going beyond and continually collapsing back into itself' (E/O 1:58) in the bid to 'discover something that thought itself cannot think' (PF 37). One way to read this is that the subject

---

5 Tony Myers, www.lacan.com\zizek – Slavoj Zizek Chronology – Key Ideas

wants to be fully present to himself, yet cannot precisely because he is constituted by the field of language, that is, the Other; hence Kierkegaard argues that the subject fears a 'difference' within, which 'cannot be grasped securely' (PF 45). The paradox of thought's wilful downfall is therefore not simply to discover what cannot be thought, but more specifically, to think the self free of lack [*savn*] (PF 39). And for this reason Climacus says: in using language the subject 'is not merely himself' (PF 37).

Shakespeare's astute commentary on this aspect of *Fragments* rightly emphasizes how Climacus is quick to situate this problematic in the context of 'erotic love': 'A person lives undisturbed in himself, and then awakens the paradox of self-love as love for another, for one missing' (PF 39); the importance of which is twofold. First, it is precisely one's inability to grasp oneself 'securely' that propels the subject to seek what is lacking, in another. One can phrase this precisely in Lacanian terms: the lack [*savn/manqué*] created through language provides the motor of desire which always points beyond itself in a process of constant deferral, or 'Man's desire is desire for the Other' (SXI 235), a point not lost on Shakespeare (Shakespeare, 2002, p. 199); second, it follows from this that Kierkegaard provides in advance of Lacan a critique of the narcissistic ego (erotic self-love) rooted in language. However, whereas the 'difference within' is for Lacan merely the prelude to the ceaseless slippage of the signifier and hence despairing resignation, for Kierkegaard it becomes the very motor of love. For Kierkegaard, the 'difference within' stops at no one particular person, but extends to all and is informed by all. Thus, what remains for Lacan a shattered dream of wholeness becomes in Kierkegaard's eyes an opening to participation in all, or the means to mutate self-love of the ego into love of others, by being rooted in desire for God.

Fifth, Lacan and Kierkegaard both refuse the notion of an underlying substantial self. Lacan's claim that 'the subject constitutes himself out of the effects of the signifier' (SXI 126) is a counter claim against any view that posits a 'living substratum'

(SXI 126) to the self; the self does not *precede* language but arises *subsequent* to language: 'by being born with the signifier, the subject is born divided. The subject is an emergence which, just before, as subject, was nothing, but which having scarcely appeared, solidifies into a signifier' (SXI 199). Is this not also precisely Kierkegaard's point? Selfhood is not a given but arises out of the contradiction between language and actuality. Before the subject has ascended to language, consciousness can only be qualified as 'possibility' (JC 168). Indeed, as Shakespeare argues: 'To the rhetorical question of whether consciousness could remain in immediate unrelatedness, Johannes answers "This is a foolish question, because if it could, there would be no consciousness at all"' (Shakespeare, 2002, p. 59; JC 167). In other words, prior to language one cannot speak of consciousness, consciousness arises subsequent to language, but only on the basis of '*pre*-supposing' (JC 167) what it cannot comprehend (actuality).

Sixth, both Kierkegaard and Lacan argue for the primacy of fragmentation. Surprisingly for Lacan fragmentation was initially allied with the fragmented body [*corps morcelé*], 'a primordial discord betrayed by the signs of malaise and motor un-coordination of the neonatal months' (E 6/96); only in later work did fragmentation come to stand for any disunity which primarily threatened the ego (SIII 39). Meanwhile Kierkegaard had already rooted our experience of fragmentation in language.

And finally, does not Kierkegaard's claim that the categories of consciousness are *trichotomous* (JC 169) precede Lacan's tri-partition of psyche? According to Lacan what distinguishes dyadic from triadic thought, that is, the imaginary from the symbolic, is the introduction of the Other. In the imaginary, relationships mutually confer a sense of wholeness on the subject; in the symbolic one is castrated and hence plagued by lack. And is this not Kierkegaard's point: that consciousness only manifests when 'interest' (*interesse* [between being]) (JC 170) in the problematic gap opened up between language and actuality is exercised? In other words, what separates triadic thought from disinterested and dyadic reflection, is an awareness of the gap opened up by language, that which Lacan calls the Other.

George Stack has argued that Kierkegaard's view that language precludes actuality spurred him on in the 'paradoxical task of trying to "show" what language would tend to hide or disguise. He did this by virtue of . . . the various stages of life, existential "categories"' (Stack, 1977, p. 61). Likewise, Nordentoft argues that Kierkegaard's indirect communication is an attempt to circumvent an epistemology which is plagued by the conflict between language and actuality (Nordentoft, 1978, pp. 331–49); while Shakespeare suggests that Kierkegaard's theory of language denies that truth can be propositional; that is, that we can simply refer to truth, and thus necessitates a subjective understanding of truth (Shakespeare, 2001, pp. 70–8). One way to paraphrase Stack, Nordentoft, and Shakespeare is to say that because Kierkegaard accepts that actuality evades us, he develops a view of truth that overrides the problem: truth is subjectivity. This is not to say that the contradiction between language and actuality is overcome; rather, Kierkegaard changes the terms within which truth is understood. In the traditional mode of understanding, what matters is objective truth; that is, truth which is open to scientific procedure, 'a kind of observation in which it is of importance that the observer be in a definite state' (CUP 52); yet even if the observer were in such a definite state or 'presuppositionless, an account would still have to be made of language' (JP 3:3281). By contrast the thesis 'truth is subjectivity' places the emphasis not on 'what' is spoken about, but 'how' it is said (CUP 202). Understood subjectively, truth concerns the subject's appropriation of one's life, and how he or she manifests it as an actuality in the choices and actions one makes. For example: the objective truth of Christianity relies on the empirical veracity of a number of claims. However, subjectively the truth is presupposed like actuality, and so what matters is how it manifests in terms of the difference it makes to a person's life in the actions and choices she or he performs. To treat truth subjectively is not to make a claim about the actuality of the world that is subject to empirical verification, precisely because we cannot get to the actual world; language is always in the way. To treat truth subjectively is to make it an appropriation. As I have already argued, the existential basis to truth is not lost on Lacan, and constitutes the core of his ethics of analysis: one must assume one's desire; however, I want to focus on Kierkegaard's construal of the sign and its implications in the light of Lacan's critique of religion: religion is a stop-gap against the uncertainty bequeathed by language (SVII 130). It will become visible that Kierkegaard's account of subjective truth is tied to the interpretive demands of the sign's ambiguity, a feature shared with Lacan; yet where Lacan takes religion as a knee-jerk reaction to semiotic uncertainty and the ensuing anxiety, Kierkegaard takes Christianity as the only means by which one can be truly uncertain.

Christ as the Sign

In *Training in Christianity* Kierkegaard's Christian pseudonym Anti-Climacus provides a threefold reflection on the sign, its particular manifestations, and the ensuing types of contradiction, culminating in a meditation on 'Christ as sign'. To this extent it might be argued that the dialogue with semiotics is central to Christian formation. He begins with the by now familiar claim that 'a sign is the negation of immediacy' (TC 124); and this being so, meaning is inherently ambiguous:

> The striking trait is the immediate, but that I regard it as a sign . . . expresses my conception that it must signify something, but the fact that it must *signify* something means that it is something else than that which it immediately is. (TC 124)

Next, he considers a 'sign of contradiction' (TC 124), by which he means 'a sign which contains in its very constitution a contradiction' (TC 124), as is the case with irony, containing as it does a unity of jest and earnestness. In such cases it is impossible to tell directly what it means; yet the very ambiguity forces the receiver to actively engage in the interpretation (TC 125). What the sign means depends on how the subject resolves the signifier. Finally, Kierkegaard discusses the sign of contradiction in Scripture: the God-man.

> To be a sign is to be, beside what one immediately is, also another thing; to be a sign of contradiction is to be another thing which stands in opposition to what one immediately is. Immediately He is an individual man, just like other men, a lowly insignificant man; but the contradiction is *that He is God.* (TC 125)

This passage is crucial because it makes the link between the linguistic sign and God *the* sign in which the initial opposition between the sign and the immediacy of that which the sign negated is reflected in the *deepening opposition within the sign itself.* Whereas before the contradiction lay between actuality and ideality, now the contradiction lies within the sign itself; the contradiction is doubled. Of course, there is no guarantee that such a contradiction will be registered. Why should those initial disciples have believed Jesus was also God? And for this reason Kierkegaard points to the importance of miracles: miracles bring to light the contradiction. But more than that, the fact that miracles are required in the first place suggests that God cannot be directly mediated: we need an external sign to point us in the right direction. As always, Kierkegaard's comments provide a prescient critique of our contemporary situation: 'No, in the modern view everything is made as direct as putting the foot into the stocking . . . . The God-man is an individual man, not a fantastic unity' (TC 126). Moreover, miracles have existential import: by pointing to the contradiction we are drawn in and our sense of reason disturbed; the God-man appears in such a manner as to cause the absolute 'offence' (TC 86) and as such demands a response. And because in comparison to an ordinary sign the God-man brings absolute extremes together, it exercises an unmatched interpretive pull: one simply has to respond. Steven Shakespeare has aptly described this process:

The Word made flesh intensifies the paradoxical unity of real and ideal, particular and universal, temporal and eternal, which is characteristic of all language usage. It does not anchor language (particularly language about God) in a self-evident instance of absolute meaning, which closes the gap between signifier and signified. Christ, as the sign of contradiction holds the two apart to a radical degree. There is no opting out of the ambiguity of language, no encounter with a truth that is clear and fully present. (Shakespeare, 2001, p. 82)

Shakespeare neatly captures Kierkegaard's point that in Christ one confronts the absolute sign of ambiguity, one that far exceeds the ambiguity of normal signs because the sign has an internal contradiction that confounds all attempts at rational appropriation. Moreover, one should note that this is not the same as the internal contradiction present in Saussure's sign where a contradiction exists between the acoustic image, such as the word 'fox', and the concept of a fox. In Christ the sign is also a logical contradiction: Christ is both God *and* man.

It will be recalled from Chapter 2 that Lacan accepted the basic premise of structuralism: language is constituted by a system of signs, and the value of a word's meaning relies on the articulation of that sign within a system of differences. However, Lacan reworked Saussure's model of the sign. Where Saussure placed the signified (concept) above the signifier (acoustic sound or image) stressing their co-dependence, Lacan reversed the equation in an attempt to fully submit the signifier and signified to difference alone. I suggest that the *deepening opposition* met in Kierkegaard's shift from the sign to the sign of contradiction met in Christ amounts to the same deepening opposition met in Lacan's revision of Saussure. Both are motivated by a need to increase the ambiguity of the sign. In Kierkegaard's case this was to thwart rational mediation or overcoming of oppositions met in the Hegelian synthesis, thereby heightening the sign's interpretive demand. For Lacan this was to free the sign from any last vestiges of representation that might tie it to the real world and, likewise, the objectifying tendency afforded by anchoring representation in an actual world. The result is that both offer a disturbing account of the sign in which one meets with a radical ambiguity that resists any appeal to a clear and simple given, and indeed both Kierkegaard and Lacan go on to counsel against any attempt to gentrify that ambiguity.

Crucially, however, Lacan and Kierkegaard part company over the theological implications of the sign. For Lacan, the radical ambiguity of the sign underpins his clearest denouncement of religion: 'Religion in all its forms consists of avoiding this emptiness' (SVII 130); religion remains for Lacan an attempt to name the unnameable, to fill the gap that lies behind signification, thereby providing an onto-theological anchor for meaning. In this sense he differs little from Freud, as he himself recognized, repeating Freud's claim that religion is a form of obsessive neurosis (SVII 130). By contrast, Kierkegaard shows that Christ is the exemplary sign, the sign of ambiguity par excellence in which absolute opposites coincide. There is no sense in which the figure of Christ is introduced to overcome ambiguity, to secure meaning such that it may shine forth in a simple transparent fashion; Christ does not plug the gap that arises between actuality and ideality; indeed, Kierkegaard's point is the inverse: the opposition met in Christ increases the ambiguity of the sign; Christ is the absolute sign of ambiguity. Yet such ambiguity need not consign one to loss; Christ forces the earnestness of faith: the ambiguity of the sign precludes any objective mediation ensuring the subjective appropriation of truth; and in this way Christ's very ambiguity becomes an opening for the movement of faith.

One could further develop the contention that Christianity is no mere stopgap by way of 'thought's paradoxical passion'. In *Philosophical Fragments* Climacus asks:

> But what is this unknown against which the understanding in its paradoxical passion collides, and which even disturbs man and his self-knowledge? It is the unknown. But it is not a

human being, insofar as he knows man, or anything else that he knows. Therefore let us call this unknown *the god*. (PF 39)

From a Lacanian perspective this would seem to confirm the claim that where the subject encounters lack he names it God: religion names the unnameable. Indeed, Climacus does not shy away from the implications of what he says: God 'cannot be grasped securely. Every time this happens, it is basically arbitrariness, and at the very bottom of the devoutness there madly lurks the capricious arbitrariness that knows it itself has produced the god' (PF 45). If therefore the human is truly to know something of the unknown (God), he must come to understand his difference; 'What, then is the difference? Indeed, what else but sin' (PF 47). Yet we cannot know sin by ourselves; we need to be told by God that we are sinners. This introduces a further paradox: we need to know God to know that he is different; how then does the learner come to understand this paradox?

[W]e do not say that he is supposed to understand the paradox but is only to understand that this is the paradox. . . . It occurs when the understanding and the paradox happily encounter each other in the moment, when the understanding steps aside and the paradox gives itself. (PF 59)

Climacus' point is that God gives something of himself, yet that giving remains ambiguous because the thing given is never precisely known; and to this degree the gift is of itself constitutive of anxiety. Thus, contra Lacan – for whom God is a neurotic defence against the anxiety of language – it is precisely the language of God that enables us to be properly anxious because he always gives Himself in terms that bring anxiety to the fore of any encounter; yet such an encounter does not resign us to lack, but by encouraging the earnestness of faith – what Lacan calls the assumption of desire – becomes the opening *to* transcendence.

I have argued this from the perspective of Kierkegaard's linguistic thought, but is this not also the main thrust of *The*

Concept of Anxiety? Anxiety, he says, arises out of 'freedom's possibilities' (CA 155). Anxiety is a response to the limitless possibilities that are open to us in our freedom. In the task of becoming we can become anything, and that responsibility and choice is dizzying. Yet anxiety only properly takes effect in the light of revelation, when it becomes clear that a decision made in the present affects the eternity of one's being. Said otherwise, only a Christian can be properly anxious. However, from the perspective of theology, anxiety is less a psychological category than a mode of grace in which freedom is freely *given*, in the sense that freedom is constitutive *of* grace: grace is freedom; and God's call is the very calling of our freedom.

Conclusion

One may surmise four points. First, far from representing a secular challenge to theology or a demand to liberalize Christianity, the psycho linguistic critique of Freud/Lacan can itself be traced to the theological critique of idealism rooted in Chalcedonian orthodoxy: Christ is fully man and fully God; *the* sign of contradiction. Second, the deepening opposition of the sign of Christ, in contrast to ordinary signs, implies that in Christ one is brought to a crisis point of anxiety; hence Christianity is less a defence against anxiety than the only true form of anxiety, prompting the same decisive response or *moment of concluding* which stimulates for Lacan the assumption of desire. Third, what psychoanalysis takes as the alienating or fragmentary experience of language is itself the mark of God's infinite difference; thus theology is able to think the effects of castration less in terms of a necessary suppression and ensuing alienation, than of a positive embrace of a prior difference. Fourth, from the standpoint of theology, one's inability to grasp oneself 'securely' (the critique of ego-psychology) need not lead to resignation or despair, for since we are already situated within God's eternal love, it gives renewed expression to Christian love of neighbour because our very being is constantly discovered to be mediated through the Other in mutual participation of God's love. Taking all this into account, might one not surmise in a strange reversal of position, that the degree to which psychoanalysis refuses Christianity becomes the mark of its own deepening neurosis?

4

Stages on the Way from Kierkegaard to Lacan

Introduction

In this chapter I explore Kierkegaard's theory of stages: the aesthetic, ethical, and religious, with reference to Lacan's trinity: the imaginary, symbolic, and real. On this basis I offer a comparative reading of Kierkegaard's treatment of Abraham and Lacan's treatment of Antigone. What transpires is the close relationship between their respective goals: assuming one's desire (Antigone), and attaining religious subjectivity (Abraham). Such a reading challenges the usual attempts to conform Kierkegaard's stages to a developmental ego-psychology because the emphasis falls on the moment that imaginary relations and symbolic certainties are punctuated by the real (that is, the religious), opening up a space of interpretive action: the assumption of desire. And, as I will argue, it is this interpretive action which constitutes the Church. Moreover, because the Church is constituted in an interpretive act, it cannot be a matter of conforming to a fixed identity – Lacan's critique of ego-psychology. As a correlate, I also show the central role humour plays in Kierkegaard's theory of the stages, concluding that Lacan is a prime example of a humorist.

Stages

One of the prominent features of Kierkegaard's oeuvre is his theory of stages: the aesthetic, ethical, and religious. In putting forward these 'ideal presentations' Kierkegaard advances the thesis that 'the number of possible ways of existing can be profitably classified under a relatively small set of categories' (Evans, 1983, pp. 11–12). The aesthetic sphere is the realm of pleasure and gratification: 'Aesthetic existence is essentially enjoyment' (CUP 288). The paradigmatic figure of the aesthetic is Don Juan. A 'downright seducer', his love is 'sensuous . . . and according to its concept, sensuous love is not faithful but totally faithless' (E/O 1:94). Don Juan exists to serve the whim of his passions and hence for him 'everything is merely an affair of the moment' (E/O 1:94). Lacking any sense of duty or commitment, his is a singular and opportune existence brought about at the expense of others.

The ethical stage is the realm of law and duty. Rather than serve one's passions the ethicist acts with a view to what is best for everyone; and to that extent he embodies a utilitarian ethos: one acts so as to maximize the greatest happiness for the greatest number. The paradigmatic figure of the ethical is Judge William. In place of the seducer we encounter a married man, committed to his wife and mindful of the mores and customs that constitute social life. In the aesthetic stage the subject is only interested in his or her self-satisfaction; for the ethicist the goal of life is self-realization in the context of duty to others.

In the religious stage attention is turned wholly towards God: 'Religiously, the task is to comprehend that a person is nothing at all before God' (CUP 461). The paradigmatic figure of the religious is Abraham, the father of faith who in his willingness to sacrifice his son Isaac suspends ethical judgement. Abraham does not appeal to a shared sense of reason to justify an act for which the ethical expression is 'murder' (FT 30); nor does he reproach God as Kant would have, distrusting the voice. Instead Abraham sets out with Isaac in silence. For Kierkegaard, Abraham embodies the *exception to the universal*. He does not act from the standpoint of his personal passions, a selfish whim opposed to the universal; neither does he act from the standpoint of a utilitarian ethic, that is, opposed to the individual. Rather, in what amounts to a Hegelian unity of opposites, he is the exception that grounds the universal: he is the exception to the rule, yet constitutive of the rule; he is the father of faith, and yet by sacrificing Isaac he is called to renounce his paternity. For this reason Kierkegaard considers the religious stage the properly paradoxical stage.

It is not difficult to see how Kierkegaard's stages correspond to Lacan's trinity: the imaginary, symbolic, and real. The aesthetic is ruled by his passions; he has yet to yield to castration and therefore inhabits the imaginary plane. For this reason Kierkegaard's aesthetics are often seducers who, like Don Juan, hear 'only the elemental voice of passion, the play of desires, the wild noise of intoxication' (E/O 1:90); and live in 'one giddy round of pleasure' (E/O 1:90).

The ethical stage corresponds to the symbolic, hence Judge William is precisely that, *a judge*; that is, he stands for the law, the minimal condition of social life and hence that which distinguishes between the imaginary and symbolic. In the following passage Kierkegaard emphasizes the role of law, as well as its alienating effect upon the human subject:

> In my day, we studied Latin grammar with a rigour that is unknown today. From this instruction I received an impression that in a different way affected my soul similarly. Insofar as I dare attribute to myself any capacity for taking a philosophic view of things, I owe it to this impression from childhood. The unconditioned respect with which I regard the rule, the veneration I felt for it, the contempt with which I looked down on the miserable life the exception endured, the to my eyes righteous way in which it was pursued in my exercise book and always stigmatised – what else is this but the distinction that is the basis of all philosophic reflection? Under this influence, when I reflected on my father, he seemed to me to be the incarnation of the rule; what came from elsewhere was the exception insofar as it was not in harmony with his command. (E/O 2:269)

Two crucial points arise from the above passage. First, Judge William clearly moves from a reflection upon the rule of grammar to the rule of the father; that is, the rule of the father is the prohibitive rule associated with language – the Name-of-the-Father – that structures our engagement with the world. Second, acceptance of the rule brings the participant into proximity with the Other of language, the real – what Kierkegaard calls the exception – which becomes the source of antagonism and motor of desire.

Finally, the religious stage corresponds directly to the real, because in the religious sphere one identifies with the exception that grounds the rule; i.e., that which is ceded as condition of entry into the symbolic; the constitutive exception to the law. As the pseudonym Constantius says in a passage that would later influence the jurist Carl Schmitt (Schmitt, 1985, p. 15):

> the exception explains the universal and himself, and if one really wants to study the universal, one only needs to look around for a legitimate exception; he discloses everything far more clearly than the universal itself. . . . Eventually one grows weary of the incessant chatter about the universal [the ethical] and the universal repeated to the point of the most boring insipidity. There are exceptions. If they cannot be explained then the universal cannot be explained, either. Generally, the difficulty is not noticed because one thinks the universal not with passion but with superficiality. The exception, however, thinks the universal with intense passion. (R 227)

Returning to Abraham, the paradigmatic figure of the religious stage, one should identify him precisely as the exception. Hence, he is not merely outside the law in the manner of the psychotic, unable to pass through the gate and into the city; rather, he is the founder of the faith: he *initiates* the law. And for this reason Abraham is characterized by silence; it is the silence that accompanies any founding event; an event which can only subsequently struggle to find a voice. Abraham is therefore radically exterior to law to the extent he is radically interior: the exception that founds the law.

Given the relation thus far between Kierkegaard and Lacan's trinities, might one not also find an analogue in their structural aims, what Kierkegaard calls becoming subjective, and Lacan 'the assumption of desire'? In what follows I explore this contention through a comparative reading of Kierkegaard's Abraham and Lacan's Antigone, challenging the usual assumption that Kierkegaard's stages conform to an ego-psychology, as well as offering a Kierkegaardian/Lacanian view of atonement. I begin with Lacan's account of Antigone.

Antigone

Sophocles' *Antigone* tells the story of the fall of the house of Thebes. Oedipus' sons Eteocles and Polynices had fallen into conflict over who should inherit the throne. Eteocles held the throne, but was challenged by Polynices. In the ensuing battle both died, leaving the throne to their uncle Creon. Following custom, Creon accorded proper burial rites to Eteocles, who died defending the city, while denying rites to the aggressor, Polynices. However, their sister Antigone insists upon performing the burial rites for Polynices, drawing her into conflict with Creon. Creon orders her to be buried alive. In the final stages of the play Creon repents but it is too late; Antigone has hanged herself. Creon's son, Haemon, Antigone's fiancé, is driven to suicide by the discovery, and his death in turn leads Eurydice, his mother and Creon's wife, to take her life.

Lacan and Antigone: Agency vs. Determinism

The key term in Lacan's exegesis of the Greek text is *Até* – from which we derive atrocity – the 'irreplaceable word' which designates not simply the limit that human life can only briefly cross, but Antigone herself (SVII 262). In the Homeric poems *Até* represents a divine temptation, a 'temporary clouding' or bewilderment due to an entanglement with the gods (Dodds, 1953, p. 5). For example, wine can leave one in a state of *Até*, not because of some natural propensity *of* the wine, but because the gods intervene *in* the wine. In the context of the tragedians *Até* referred principally to sorrowful and disastrous events caused by the gods and wrought upon someone, usually in the context of marriage (Doyle, 1984, pp. 1–6). In both cases *Até* signifies the hand of fate and hence the role attributed to the gods. This was to be typically contrasted with the Greek *Hamartia*, a moral mistake for which the individual is the culpable agent. In Sophocles' play, *Hamartia* characterizes Creon, while *Até* characterizes Antigone. Thus the play stages the conflict between the determined actions of Antigone, and the free choices exercised by Creon.

With regard to Lacan, one should note two points. First, the association *Até* yields with regard to his existing claims about the signifier: it is the displacement of the signifier which determines the subjects in their destiny. As the bearer of *Até*, Antigone's actions seem predetermined, only not by the gods as such, but the signifiers which predetermine her place in the world, her family name for example. Here one should recall Lacan's articulation of the Freudian *Wiederholungszwang* or 'repetition compulsion' from 'The purloined letter' in conjunction with 'The circuit' (SII 77–93): the subject is placed within an existing circuit dictated by the signifying chain, and led to repeat various subjective positions (that is, a particular perspective or action) determined by the route the signifiers take. As Lacan says in regard to the chain:

Here we rediscover what I've already pointed out to you, namely that the unconscious is the discourse of the other. This discourse of the other is not the discourse of the abstract other, of the other in the dyad, of my correspondent, nor even of my slave, it is the discourse of the circuit in which I am integrated. I am one of its links. It is the discourse of my father for instance, in so far as my father made mistakes which I am absolutely condemned to reproduce ... I am condemned to reproduce them because I am obliged to pick up again the discourse he bequeathed to me, not simply because

I am his son, but because one can't stop the chain of discourse, and it is precisely my duty to transmit it in its aberrant form to someone else. (SII 89)

And this is precisely the predicament Antigone faces, compelled to act by the collective guilt of the family, the crimes of Oedipus. The ensuing self-mutilation, violence and suicide, flow from the initial distress into which she was born. For this reason Lacan highlights the Chorus' claim that she 'went in search of her family *Até*', the Other into which she has been born (SVII 277); as well as Antigone's cry: 'I am dead and I desire death', compelled as it were by the founding Oedipal murder (SVII 281). It is not without irony then that Lacan makes her and not Creon the paradigm of the ethical act *par excellence*. After all, despite his mistakes it is Creon who nonetheless *makes* mistakes. It is not the case that his actions are external to his will, such that he is guided by the gods (SVII 277); rather, he must take the final responsibility for them.

The question remains: how does Antigone assume agency for the ethical act or assume her desire? For this we must turn to the question of limits because *Até* represents for Lacan a limit that human life can only briefly cross. As William Richardson has pointed out, when Lacan speaks of crossing the limits of *Até*, one is not transgressing *Até* but the very obverse: maintaining absolute fidelity to her [f]*até*.[1] That is to say, Antigone cannot escape the collective guilt of her family – the determinative chain of signifiers – but she can as it were embrace in its entirety the collective guilt of her family and draw its 'radically destructive character' (SVII 283) to its logical conclusion, even at the expense of her own death:

Antigone appears as *autonomous*, as a pure and simple relationship of the human being to that of which he miraculously happens to be the bearer, namely, the signifying cut that confers on him the indomitable power of being what he is in the face of everything that may oppose him. (SVII 282)

1 William Richardson, Lecture notes, 8 July 2004.

In defying the decree of Creon she assumes fully the crime of Oedipus from whose incestuous union sprang two brothers, Eteocles, who comes to represent power, and the criminal Polynices. Antigone becomes 'purely and simply the guardian of the being of the criminal as such' (SVII 283), that is, her family *Até*.

Lacan and Antigone: Tragedy and Beauty

Lacan's employment of Antigone highlights the relation between the experience of psychoanalysis and tragedy with a view to the direction of treatment. As he says: '*Antigone* is a tragedy, and tragedy is in the forefront of our experience as analysts' (SVII 243). The key to this relationship lies in the word 'catharsis' or 'purgation'. Aristotle had used the word to denote tragedy: 'A tragedy . . . is the imitation of an action that is serious and also . . . complete in itself . . . with incidents arousing fear and pity, wherewith to accomplish its catharsis of such emotions' (Aristotle, 1984, 1449b). Breuer and Freud adopted this term as the goal of therapy: where unconscious mental processes were being directed into bodily symptoms (conversion hysteria), the goal is an abreaction or discharge of the pathogenic effects (Laplanche, 1988, pp. 60–1).

However, one must be careful to clarify what Lacan means by purgation, and how Antigone effects purgation. According to Lacan, it is Antigone's dazzling splendour which purges the reader: 'Catharsis is the beauty effect' (SVII 286). But why does Antigone shine with blinding beauty? For Lacan 'the beauty effect derives from the relationship of the hero to the limit, which is defined on this occasion by a certain *Até* (SVII 286). That is to say, it is the appropriation by Antigone of her family [f]*até* that renders her dazzling because in accepting her [f]*até* she willingly manifests the desire for death (i.e. the death drive). Her desire to assume responsibility for her family is expressed in her willingness to die.

But why should death render her the image of splendour and

dazzling beauty? A clue is given by Lacan's reference to the Kantian sublime (SVII 286). The novelty of Kant's sublime lies in its relation to representation. The sublime is that which remains both within and outside of representation. For example, nature elicits the sublime to the extent it shines forth its vast magnitude which is both represented yet that which exceeds our imagination. In discerning the sublime the mind is therefore caught in alternating currents of repulsion and attraction which contravene the categories of judgement; the subject encounters a point of excess and this point threatens to swallow the subject.

In desiring death Antigone incarnates the sublime, bringing into representation that which cannot be represented: death. Through her fidelity to the family *Até*, she makes visible the one thing that cannot be made visible. As Lacan says: 'The moving side of beauty causes all critical judgment to vacillate, stops analysis and plunges the different forms involved into a certain confusion or, rather, an essential blindness' (SVII 281). To put it in terms of the Lacanian triad, her desire for death shatters the imaginary, incarnating the real within the symbolic.

And it is the dazzling effect of beauty which causes purgation by bringing the real into speech; that is, manifesting the very lack upon which subjectivity is founded. As Lacan says, 'we are purged, purified of everything of that order. And that order, we can now immediately recognise, is properly speaking the order of the *imaginary*. We are purged of it' (SVII 248; italics mine).

Yet crucially, what enables her to manifest the sublime is the extent to which her desire is manifest in action, or in Kierke-gaardian terms, she appropriates her desire subjectively. And this is the point that the question of the analyst and analysand, agency and determinism, tragedy and beauty, overlap.

Antigone exemplifies the subject who is able to assume her desire: that is to say, she is able to relate her action to her desire, regardless of the injunctions made upon her by Creon and the symbolic. And this is the goal of analysis. Yet this is achieved only at the expense of the symbolic, only by crossing over into the real, by situating oneself in the realm of trauma. As Žižek puts it, 'there is no ethical act proper without taking the risk of such a momentary 'suspension of the big Other', of the socio-symbolic network that guarantees the subject's identity' (Žižek, 2000b, pp. 263–4).

As the analyst, she helps the analysands (that is, the audience) purge themselves, and she achieves this dramatically because she manifests through action that which cannot be represented, death. Likewise, it is the analyst's task to bring to bear upon the analysand the central and constitutive lack upon which we are founded (what Lacan terms *das Ding*).

The Act

What then is the relation between the cathartic effect or purgation, and assuming agency? By encountering the trauma of the real, by being literally re-traumatized, one shatters the neurotic defences against trauma. The suspension of the symbolic and subsequent encounter with the real opens up a space in which one can act, reconfiguring the past with a view to action in the present. The double wound destabilizes one's ground of experience, but thereby opens it up for renewal. As Lacan says:

[It is] when the traumatic elements – grounded in an image which has never been integrated, draw near that holes, points of fracture appear in the unification, the synthesis of the subject's history. I have pointed out how in starting from these holes that the subject can realign himself within the different symbolic determinations which make him a subject with a history. (SI 197)

And this is the basis of the analytic cure: where a traumatic experience has led to neurosis, the means to free the subject involves a further trauma. This method finds a curious analogy in *Asterix and the Big Fight*. When Obelix renders Getafix the Druid senseless having accidentally knocked him over the head with a menhir, he reasons that a second blow may well restore Getafix's sense (Goscinny and Uderzo, 1974). Said otherwise, through the identification with the real, one is able to commit an *act*. What then precisely is an act? An act is an assumption of agency by the analysand which is not circumscribed by the symbolic or in clinical terms by the neurotic's defences; an act breaks with the symbolic and yet it is not opposed, because the act is also a constitutive moment of the symbolic, reshaping the symbolic. And for this reason the act is existential. As Žižek puts it, in the act one grasps the symbolic 'in the mode of becoming' (Žižek, 1996, p. 147). The act is therefore both inside and outside the structure or field it gives rise to, occupying a position of what Lacan calls, 'extimacy' (SVII 139).

As Rex Butler says, the act is not simply a moment of potentiality, to be manifest as actual; the undecided potentiality of the act becoming decided through its symbolic formation (Butler, 2005, p. 68); this being the case one would fall back into the type of metaphysics criticized by Kierkegaard in which the world is an inevitable unfolding of prior givens; and all the risk, uncertainty, and passion of existence is drained out. Rather, the act opens up an area of undecidability in an area that was decided (Butler, 2005, p. 68). And for this reason one can say in Kierkegaardian terms that the act marks the transition from objectivity to subjectivity, from the ethical to the religious.

Abraham and Antigone

Lacan's reading of Antigone gives us a clue to reading Kierkegaard's *Fear and Trembling*. Instead of situating the work in terms of Kierkegaard's developmental schemes or stages, one should simply substitute Antigone for Abraham. From this perspective Kierkegaard presents the story of Abraham as a Lacanian tragedy in which Abraham crosses over the limit of *Até* and thereby performs a purgative effect on the reader.

Like Antigone, Abraham maintains an unconditional fidelity to God's command: 'Take your son, your only child, whom you love, and go to the land of Moriah. There you shall offer him as a burnt offering' (Gen. 22.2). Abraham's willingness to kill his son becomes the expression of his desire for God. In other words, Abraham achieves the goal of analysis: the assumption of desire; manifest in his unflinching desire for death, his willingness to murder (the ethical expression of the act) his only and beloved son: Isaac.

Kierkegaard's meditation on Abraham renders him a tragic figure, and Christianity a tragic religion; tragic in the sense that they purge the participant. Abraham becomes tragic by incarnating death in the symbolic through his willing desire to kill Isaac. Emphasizing this dimension of the story Kierkegaard renders Christianity tragic by bringing to bear upon the reader the *real* of Christianity: that the father of faith was a murderer. Yet like the analyst, this scandalous reversal reaffirms Christianity as an act. In other words, Kierkegaard's aim is to traumatize the Christian reader, and through that trauma seek the renewal of Christianity. As Žižek says: Kierkegaard's suspension of the ethical 'reaffirm[s] the Christian attitude in its "scandalous" reverse, before it settled down into a force of law and order, i.e., to reaffirm it as an *act*' (Žižek, 2001, p. 83).

Indeed, this was Kierkegaard's stated aim. Kierkegaard diagnosed the nineteenth-century treatment of Christianity as a 'delusion' (POV 53), a neurotic defence against actually being Christian. According to Kierkegaard Christianity was being treated as an object open to scientific observation by detached observers – as witnessed with today's quest for the historical Jesus – or subjected to the dictates of a universal reason. Yet the more objectively true Christianity became (i.e. imaginary), the more it ceased to become Christian because the truth of Christianity was not to be found in speculation, but embodied action: 'being a Christian should be the most mature and most self-conscious decision' (JP 1:390).

Contrast Kierkegaard's Abraham to Kant's. On the basis of universal reason Kant condemned Abraham's action: 'Abraham should have replied to this supposedly divine voice: "That I ought not to kill my son is quite certain. But that you, this apparition, are God – of that I am not so certain"' (Kant, 1979,

p. 115). Kant plays the part of Creon, embodying a utilitarian ethic because if parents were to act upon a voice asking them to sacrifice their children, society would fall into chaos. Likewise, Creon's initial decision is in perfect conformity with the law of the *polis*. In condemning the one, Kant and Creon maintain the order of the many: the exception is sacrificed for the norm. Meanwhile Kierkegaard's Abraham embodies the exception (FT 78) through his fidelity to an act whose outcome is logically death.

And for this reason Abraham is not to be confused with the psychotic as René Rasmussen has suggested. According to Rasmussen, Abraham is outside the law, commanded by a voice to undertake the worst possible crime. And Abraham 'talks like a psychotic subject occasionally does, in tongues, or as Kierkegaard says: "in a divine Tongue"' (Rasmussen, 2005, p. 113). Arguably she fails to take into account the specificity of Kierkegaard's reading. For Kierkegaard, what matters is not the voice as such, so much as the silence which accompanies Abraham's act; and in accordance with his thesis – *truth is subjectivity* – it is Abraham's action rather than voice which do the talking. The action speaks the manifestation of desire, and thus introduces a sudden reverse. Abraham *acts*, he suspends symbolic certainties and in doing so he founds a faith, yet what is given remains undecidable.

Christ and Antigone

On this basis can one say that Lacan's account of Antigone is almost Christian; and hence analysis a parody of theology? For example, does not Christ incarnate the death drive in his relentless push to Jerusalem, 'the city that kills the prophets' (Matt. 23.37)? And despite Peter's protestations Christ becomes as Antigone, the self-willed victim, willingly giving himself over to the chief priests and the scribes to be condemned to death (Mark 10.33). And like Antigone, Christ is caught in a family drama in which his actions are utterly determined (born to die);

yet he assumes the act of absolute agency, as the fresco in the Monastero di Sant' Antonio in Polesine in Ferrara suggests. Here we find a graphic representation of Christ climbing the cross in a desolate desert, with no one around. And where Antigone becomes 'the guardian of the being of the criminal' by assuming family responsibility for her brother, and by extension the murderous and incestuous act of Oedipus, does not Christ more generally become the guardian of the being of humanity, assuming the [f]*até* of mankind? Being human he is bound by mortality, a consequence of the fall (Gen. 2.17), yet he assumes the [f]*até* of humankind at the expense of his own life, crossing over the limit and thereby playing out humanity's hand to the end. And like Lacan's Antigone who 'perpetuates, eternalises, immortalises that *Até*' (SVII 283), Christ wins eternity for humankind. By assuming his desire, the desire for death (that is, willingly going to his death), Christ incarnates the real in the symbolic; Christ assumes the image of splendour, the narrative allure drawn from his dazzling beauty, itself a product of his desire for death.

Finally, do not Christ and Antigone both embody the logic of exception? Antigone does so because she chooses the exception to Creon's Law, thereby transcending the ethical; Christ because his death was not that of a martyr to a higher truth, but the very truth for which others would become martyrs.

Such a reading should critique in advance any suggestion that Christ's death leans towards the suicidal. Christ's point is not to exit the symbolic into the real, but rather manifest the real *in* the symbolic through his action. In this way Christ assumes the status of the sublime object, short-circuiting the real and the symbolic, and in bringing the real into the symbolic he *traumatizes* us, breaking through the wall of language. One should be careful to observe that the split is not at the level of reality and its underlying support whereby Christ stands in *for* God, just as Christ is not a man transcendentally supported by God (the humanist or liberal reading); rather the split is inherent to Christ himself: Christ *is* God *and* man, and in reading the Gospels one is purged through the confrontation with the real;

Christ performing the function of the analyst, bringing the real of experience to bear upon the follower. The imaginary, that is, our narcissistic identifications, are punctuated through the encounter with Christ. And it is perhaps for this reason Lacan would say some years later: '*The gods belong to the field of the real*' (SXI 45).

Finally, by exposing us to the trauma of the real, one is invited into a moment of interpretive practice which allows one to enter a participatory atonement through the ecclesial practice of exegetical openness. The Church produces a saviour in and through its interpretive creativity. In other words, Jesus founds the Church not by providing an identity to conform to, but by clearing a path, creating an opening of interpretive potency, a path the way of which cannot be known in advance. So participation is precisely the co-creativity in this interpretive moment.

The Exception to the Exception

The difference of course between Antigone and Christ, as Kierkegaard understood it, was that in Christ one encounters *absolute* suffering and *absolute* agency in the manner that Christ is not half-God/half-man but wholly God *and* wholly man. Moreover, Christ assumes responsibility for all of humanity, as opposed to his immediate kin because we are all his immediate kin. And for this reason Christ exceeds all aesthetic categories such as the tragic. In a similar manner Christ cannot be so easily situated in the logic of exception. As John Milbank has argued, Christ is not merely an exception, but *the* exception to the exception. On the one hand he is what Georgio Agamben has identified as *homo sacer*, utterly 'abandoned by the disciples; given up by the Sanhedrin, passed between Pilate and Herod, to be finally given a Roman execution (Milbank, 2003, p. 82); the sovereign victim who 'died as three times excluded: by the Jewish law of its tribal nation; by the Roman universal Law of Empire; by the democratic will of the mob', thereby summing up the entire history of human polity: the tribe, the universal absolute state, and the democratic consensus (Milbank, 2003, p. 96). On the other hand Christ could never be abandoned because Christ *is* God. And as for the cry of dereliction in Matthew 27.46 and Mark 15.34, that is not the cry of abandonment but the point at which Christ fully experiences the self-separation of sinful humanity from God; hence it is to God (*Ελωί*), not the Father (*Πάτερ*) of Luke 23.46 to whom he commits his spirit, that Christ in his humanity cries out (Milbank, 2003, pp. 98–9).

In other words, in Christ we encounter the absolute coincidence of oppositions without residue or gap between the enunciator and the enunciated. As Kierkegaard notes, he does not bring a message, he *is* the message. Therefore Christianity does leave one simply to oscillate between the norm (the symbolic) and its exception (real), trapped within a melancholic law that is haunted by its own absence. However, since Christ is the exception to the exception, his death is the death of death, and so what is most excluded, that is, in the place of death, becomes life. In this way the analysand makes the transition described by Kierkegaard, from anxiety to grace.

The Funny Thing about Lacan . . .

Given that psychoanalysis is a parody of Christianity, Lacan is best described in terms of Kierkegaard's humorist. For Kierkegaard the humorist occupies a '*confinium* [border]' between the stages: 'There are three existence-spheres: the aesthetic, the ethical, the religious. To these there is a respectively corresponding *confinium*: irony is the *confinium* between the aesthetic and the ethical; humour is the *confinium* between the ethical and religious' (CUP 501–2). Why is humour not a sphere in its own right? C. Stephen Evans argues that what separates the boundary position from the stages is that they are not universal types, but require a specific intellect (Evans, 1983, pp. 185–205). The aesthetic, ethical, and religious do not require any particular intellect. However, Kierkegaard distinguishes between the educated religious person and the simple religious person, who achieves what the educated does only more directly: 'What the simple religious person does directly, the simple religiously *aware* person does only through humour' (CUP 179; italics mine). In other words, the two transitional stages are added for the more educated. If there was something specifically to gain from these zones they would amount to a case of favouritism. However, first, Kierkegaard's point seems to be that they merely accommodate to the more reflective person, in other words, when the understanding leaps ahead of the practice the subject can be described as either ironic or humorous, thus the border describes the point where the intellectual gives primacy to thought, paralysing the practical. In irony, the subject gains the intellectual understanding of the 'ethical infinite requirement' (CUP 502) in relation to the finitude of the aesthetic. Irony expresses the contradiction between knowing what to do in the ethical yet remaining in aesthetic categories. Humour expresses the contradiction between gaining an intellectual understanding of Christianity, yet remaining in ethical categories:

Humour, when it uses Christian categories (sin, forgiveness of sin, atonement, God in time, etc.), is not Christianity but a pagan speculative thought that has come *to know* all the essentially Christian. It can come deceptively close to the essentially Christian, but at the point where the decision captures [*fange*], at the point where existence captures the existing person, just as when the table captures [*Bordet fanger*] when a card is played, so that he must remain in existence, while the bridge of recollection and immanence behind is demolished . . . – at that point humour is not present'. (CUP 272)

5

Full and Empty Speech

Introduction

In Lacan's early work, most notably 'The Rome discourse' (E 40:247), but also in *Seminar I*, the goal of analysis is spoken of in terms of the distinction *full and empty speech*. As I argue in this chapter, these two categories are nascent in Kierkegaard's work, corresponding to his distinction between a subjective and objective approach to the question of truth, which in turn arises from his critique of a passionless and nominal Christianity. Mediating the two is Heidegger. By tracing the continuity between Heidegger and some key areas of Lacanian analysis, I strengthen the contention of the previous chapter that Lacan views the end point of analysis in similar terms to the way Kierkegaard views the religious stage.

Having consolidated the relation between their prospective goals, I then move on to explore their respective use of humour in procuring that end. By highlighting their affinity I show the merit of Kierkegaard's work for clinical practice.

Finally, I show how Kierkegaard situates his practice in analogical terms to God's engagement with the world. This allows me to construe God as the 'arch-analyst' and analysis a form of analogical participation in God's creative work: a work of love in which, like God, the analyst establishes a realm of created independence to help the subject engage in the subjective appropriation of truth.

Kierkegaard: Subjective and Objective Truth

For Kierkegaard there are two types of disposition or reflection adopted in regard to truth. By truth he means those thoughts and beliefs that are 'related essentially to existence' (CUP 199n.); that is, those ideas that shape our fundamental view of the world and exercise a meaningful effect on how we choose to comport ourselves. These dispositions are subjective or objective reflections. This means that given a statement like 'Christ has risen', one may reflect upon it objectively or subjectively. Kierkegaard is not concerned with making a distinction between objective and subjective *truth* here, but the type of reflection we bring to bear upon essential truth, truth that has ethical consequences for the way we live.

When the truth is reflected upon objectively, it is treated '*as an object to which the knower relates himself. What is reflected upon is not the relation but that what he relates himself to is the truth, the true*' (CUP 199; italics in original). Objective reflection is therefore 'indifferent to the thinking subject' (CUP 72–3); it tends towards the object and away from the subject, hence it is associated with detached scientific observation (CUP 52).

If '*Objectively the emphasis is on **what** is said; subjectively the emphasis is on **how** it is said*' (CUP 202; italics and emphasis in original). Objective truth renders the subject redundant by leading away from him to the object of knowledge; subjective reflection retains an awareness of the subject and how he is related to what is under discussion. Thus the subjective thinker must undertake the task of consciously relating him or herself to essential truth. Or as Kierkegaard says: 'the development of subjectivity consists precisely in this, that he, acting, works through himself in his thinking about his own existence, consequently that he actually thinks what is thought by actualising it' (CUP 169). This is the meaning of Kierkegaard's celebrated claim that 'truth is subjectivity' (CUP 189): ethical and religious questions require an answer that engages one's subjectivity; that is, one must respond with a passionate inwardness; passion

being the interest of the self, directed towards an ethical existence (CUP 312–13).

Lacan: Empty and Full Speech

In his early period, Lacan worked within the opposition of
empty and full speech. Empty speech is speech situated along
the imaginary axis. For Lacan, subjectivity is founded upon
identification with a false image of unity. The subject perpetuates this imaginary self by choosing relationships which confer
upon him or herself the sense of sameness, relations which are
in effect 'narcissistic embraces' (E 42/249). This is because it is
far easier to construct oneself on the basis of another, incorpo-
rating his or her tastes and desires, rather than confront the lack
that resides in each of us. And because the subject has con-
structed him or herself upon the basis of another, he or she is
unable to enjoin in the assumption of desire [*l'assomption de
son désir*]' (E 46/254). In other words, in constructing our
desires on the basis of another we reinforce our alienation from
our desire. As Lacan says: 'For in the work he does to recon-
struct it *for another*, he encounters anew the fundamental alienation that made him construct it *like another*, and that has
always destined it to be taken from him *by another*' (E 42/249;
italics in original).

This is the meaning of Lacan's enigmatic phrase, 'Man's
desire is desire of the Other' (SXI 235), we desire what the other
desires. Speech is empty therefore to the extent that it is ironi-
cally filled by the other. As Lee puts it: 'From the subject's own
perspective, then, his speech has been in an important sense
"empty": it has been emptied of the subject by being filled with
his alienating *moi* [ego] identity' (Lee, 1990, p. 40). In a clinical
setting, a subject whose speech is empty will tend to objectify
himself in the following ways: 'I think that I'm the kind of
person . . .', or alternatively, 'my teacher thinks that I'm . . .'
(Nobus, 2000, p. 65). The art of analysis is to break the
analysand's imaginary identifications, 'suspending the subject's

certainties until their final mirages have been consumed' (E 44/251).

It is not difficult to see how empty speech corresponds to the objective standpoint. The objective standpoint seeks to ground itself in sure and certain foundations; it relies on a universally accepted standard of rationality, so that given the same premise we can all arrive at the same conclusion, thereby conferring a collective self-same identity and propagating the illusion of the whole. As Kierkegaard says: 'the objective way is of the opinion that it has the security that the subjective way does not have' (CUP 194) because our thoughts are buttressed by a collective other.

The convergence of Lacan and Kierkegaard on empty speech or the objective standpoint can also be traced through their mutual critique of Hegel. From Kierkegaard's perspective, Hegel's system was all that was wrong with recollection and by the same token objective reflection. It was a philosophy of immanence in which truth was mediated through a progressive and unfolding rationality. Moreover, it assumed a level of knowledge logically only tenable to a god, rather than an actually existing German philosopher. By contrast, Kierkegaard wanted to say that God is transcendent, untenable to shared rationality, and constantly recalls us to our contingent existence.

Likewise, when Lacan comes to criticize Hegel in 'Subversion of the subject' he argues that Hegel's thought is all that is wrong with the doctrine of recollection:

[L]et us re-examine from this angle the service we expect from Hegel's phenomenology: that of marking out an ideal solution – one that involves a permanent revisionism, so to speak, in which what is disturbing about truth is constantly being reabsorbed, truth being in itself but what is lacking in the realisation of knowledge. The antinomy the scholastic tradition posited as principal is here taken to be resolved by virtue of being *imaginary*. *Truth is nothing but what knowledge can learn that it knows merely by putting its ignorance to work* . . . This dialectic is convergent and proceeds to the conjuncture defined as absolute knowledge. As it is deduced, this conjuncture can only be the conjuncture of the symbolic with the real from which nothing more can be expected. What is this if not a subject finalised in his self-identity? From which one can conclude that this subject is already perfect(ed) here and is the fundamental hypothesis of the entire process. (E 285/797–8; italics mine)

Hegel's work implies an imaginary identification at the level of epistemology because knowledge is already known; it is immanent, discovered through the convergent dialectic which raises the subject above contingent existent to absolute knowledge.

In contrast to Hegel and his underlying doctrine of recollection, Lacan had already aligned himself with Augustine's *De Magistro*. In this work Augustine responds to the Socratic dilemma concerning learning: 'One can never find out anything new: either one knows it already, in which case there is no need to find it, or else one does not and in that case there is no means of recognising it when found' (Plato, 1981, p. 104). The doctrine of recollection attends to this paradox. It holds that the soul is immortal and in the course of its transmigration through the cosmos has learnt everything; all knowledge is therefore situated latent in the mind. Learning is a matter of recollecting or remembering what is latent – the basis of self-knowledge; and teaching is a matter of midwifery.

Augustine's rejection of this doctrine is staged in terms of the debate on signs between Augustine and his son Adeonatus. According to Augustine, only God can be the ultimate cause of man's acquisition of truth in the learning process because while we cannot learn anything without signs, signs cannot teach us everything because no meaning is ever exhaustive. Likewise, words cannot make us see truths intelligible to the mind. Therefore we rely on the interior teacher Christ – the *Word* – to mediate the truth, through words. The difference between Plato and Augustine was therefore that for the Christian, enlightenment arises from a non-human source (God) rather than immanently discerned (recollection); nonetheless it requires an intermediary (language) which is accessible to both the senses and the mind (Augustine, 1950, pp. 129–53).

Augustine's argument was important over and against Hegel from Lacan's point of view, because it chimed with his own claim that language was the condition of its own impossibility, it was the medium of truth, yet simultaneously undermined the truth process because it places everything under the machinations of the sign. But also for the reasons established by Kierkegaard: recollection stands on the side of eternity rather than contingent existence, slipping out of time into the realm of eternally fixed virtues and ideas thereby abstracting from the process of becoming and presupposing the subject already finalized in their identity. Indeed, to underline the point, Lacan would go on to expressly situate the doctrine of recollection within the imaginary, while directly referring to Kierkegaard:

> Freud distinguishes two completely different structurations of human experience – one which, along with Kierkegaard, I call *ancient*, based on reminiscence, presupposing agreement, harmony between man and the world of his objects, which means that he recognises them, because in some way he has already known them. (SII 100)

For this reason Lacan sided early on with the scholastic tradition, and ultimately Kierkegaard, because it afforded an emphasis on the subject established in the future anterior, a subject in a process of becoming, moving towards God yet without becoming gods in the process; a way of danger and of uncertainty.

Full Speech

In contrast to the timelessness of the imaginary, full speech is speech in the mode of the future anterior; speech which reflects the historical temporality of the self remaining open to constant revision. As with Heidegger's use of the future anterior, it calls for the exercise of an 'authentic attitude of care', an existential appropriation of one's history, a sense of agency. For this reason Lacan says: 'Full speech is speech which performs'; that is, it is speech manifest through action. Moreover, this sentiment did not diminish. In his 1959–60 seminars on *Ethics* Lacan would again make action a central component of the analytic goal in his injunction: 'Have you acted in conformity with the desire that is in you?' (SVII 314).

It is then not difficult to see how full speech constitutes in Kierkegaardian terms, the subjective appropriation of truth. Indeed, in *The Concept of Anxiety*, the pseudonym Vigilius Haufniensis characterizes the bondage of sin precisely in terms of the distance between speech and action. He uses the image of two people concealed under a cloak in which one speaks and the other acts, without any relation between the two (CA 118–19). Sin manifests in terms of a life in which speech is unable to realize its potential in decisive action, and for this reason Kierkegaard says: 'action to subjectivity' (CUP 339).

Heidegger

One should strengthen the relation between Kierkegaard and Lacan's categories by pointing to the mediating role Heidegger plays apropos chatter and speech. In *The Present Age* Kierkegaard charges a bureaucratic society with dehumanizing people, a process he calls 'levelling', by which individuals are made to feel secure only in mass. In the process of levelling, individuality is abolished. Levelling is accompanied by characteristic effects such as 'chatter' in which the vital distinction between the time for speech and time for silence is lost. Moreover, the process of levelling '*hinders* and *stifles* all action' (PA 51), it exalts the category of generation over individuality (PA 52), 'reflection' over 'action of the individual' (PA 54), and ushers in an age of passionless understanding, which abolishes the principle of contradiction. Of chatter Kierkegaard writes:

It is the result of doing away with the vital distinction between talking and keeping silent. Only someone who knows how to remain essentially silent can really talk – and act essentially. Silence is the essence of inwardness, of the inner life. Mere gossip anticipates real talk, and to express what is still in thought weakens action by forestalling it . . . When mere scope is concerned, talkativeness wins the day, it jabbers on incessantly about everything and nothing. When people's attention is no longer turned inwards, when they are no longer satisfied with their own inner lives, but turn to others and to things outside themselves, where the relation is intellectual, in search of that satisfaction. [. . .] that is the time for talkativeness. . . . But talkativeness is afraid of the silence which reveals its emptiness. (PA 69)

Arguably it was this distinction between chatter and speech that formed the basis of Heidegger's distinction between idle talk (*Gerede*) and discourse (*Rede*), and Heidegger's related term *Einebnen* [levelling] (Macey, 1988, pp. 147–8). Idle talk fails to draw the speaker or listener into the creative possibilities of language, failing to invoke the force of words, the possibility of interpretation to enlighten and open up new pathways of thinking. By contrast, in 'discourse' communication is full of concern; discourse brings those involved to participate in the disclosure of Being which means to take into account our historical nature and its creative possibilities (Heidegger, 1962, pp. 211–14).

It is from here a short step to Lacan and empty speech whereby one constructs oneself for another, that is to say, one is levelled. Only in full speech does one bring the Other to bear on speech, what Kierkegaard calls 'silence', and with that the existential concern marked by decisive action.

In *Postscript*, Climacus suggests that 'the Socratic inwardness of existing is an analogue to faith' (CUP 205). In other words, experientially there is little difference between the Christian and the more general subject who is existentially engaged in the question of truth. On that basis, and given the relation between

Lacan and Kierkegaard, can we not speak of the goal of analysis in terms of an analogue of faith?

Procuring Subjectivity

Kierkegaard was not just concerned for the Christian nominalism of Hegel, but for the nominalism of Copenhagen where even the wife of a civil servant could declare herself Christian simply on the basis of nationality (CUP 51). In order to procure a subjective disposition in his general readers, Kierkegaard employed a form of 'indirect communication', writing under the guise of various pseudonyms, a practice not uncommon in the literature of the feuilleton (Patterson, 2002, pp. 25–49). The pseudonyms are not simply pen names but independent fictitious characters in their own right; they have their own views and styles, contributing to a gallery of voices and opinions to the extent that Kierkegaard wrote: 'in the pseudonymous books there is not a single word by me. I have no opinion about them except as a third party, no knowledge of their meaning except as a reader, nor the remotest private relation to them' (CUP 626). The pseudonyms depict the various aspects or stages of existence: the aesthetic, ethical, and religious. Their aim is to make readers aware of their own nature and their shortcomings by holding up a mirror to them, thereby encouraging them to reach a decision about how they live their life. The most striking example of the pseudonymous intent is *Either/Or*, where the aesthetic lifestyle is counterposed to the ethical life. Which life is better to take? The book refuses sides, leaving the reader to decide. To this extent they are reproductions of Socrates' maieutic skill, forcing the reader or listener to become active in the interpretation (JP 4:4266).

In particular, the pseudonyms are used to provoke 'the most inward qualification of the essentially Christian' (MWA 5), although this is by no means the stated purpose or topic of the conversations. Kierkegaard justified the deception because he saw the problem of Christianity viewed objectively in terms of an 'illusion' or 'delusion' (POV 53), and that:

> an illusion can never be removed directly . . . . By a direct attack he only strengthens a person in the illusion and also infuriates him. Generally speaking, there is nothing that requires as gentle a treatment as the removal of an illusion. (POV 43)

Thus he employs a kind of benevolent deception:

> It means that one does not begin directly with what one wishes to communicate but begins by taking the other's delusion at face value. Thus one does not begin . . . in this way: I am a Christian, you are not a Christian . . . one begins this way: Let us talk about the aesthetic. The deception consists in one's speaking this way precisely in order to arrive at the religious. (POV 54)

Kierkegaard's reference to Socratic maieutics points to the affinity his pseudonymous style has with the role of the analyst. As Lacan says:

> Psychoanalysis is a dialectic . . . *an art of conversation.* The art of conversation of Socrates in *Meno* is to teach the slave to give his own speech its true meaning . . . . In other words, the position of the analyst must be that of an *ignorantia docta*, which does not mean knowing [*savante*], but formal, and what is capable of being formative for the subject. (SI 278)

Moreover, in the light of ego-psychology, maieutics bears on two crucial points. First, it ensures that the analysand does not identify with the analyst and thus reinstate imaginary relations, constructing himself on the basis of another; rather, the analysand is forced to make a decision about his life based upon his desire. Second, analytic neutrality precludes normative assumptions being made by the analyst, because should the analyst assume himself as normative, he will inevitably recreate the analysand in his own image, devolving analytic relations into formal relations of power (E 216/586).

Kierkegaard's use of pseudonyms, or 'armed neutrality' (AN 127) as he also referred to it, directly addresses these same two concerns. He values Socratic maieutics for its ability in making the reader 'himself active' (JP 4:4266) while neutralizing the role of the analyst. He also displays a marked sensitivity to the dynamics of power in such a relationship:

> It is not now up to me, a human being, to judge others, particularly not in the role of one who knows human hearts, which here would have to be the case. If I were now to insist that I am a Christian, what would this mean in the situation? It would mean that I am a Christian in contrast to Christians – that is, that I am a Christian raised to the second power, the distinguished Christian. This is why I keep it neutral with regard to my being a Christian (AN 139).

Analytic or armed neutrality becomes a point of ethics for Kierkegaard, pertaining to an act of humility inasmuch as the analyst is not presumptuous about his own distinguished status.

However, there is a more practical reason for the indirect approach acknowledged by Kierkegaard and Lacan that pertains to the nature of defence. For Kierkegaard, as previously stated, inducing Christianity as a subjective experience was akin to removing an illusion, however, 'an illusion can never be removed directly . . . . By a direct attack he only strengthens a person in the illusion' (POV 43). This concern is powerfully captured by a case study referred to Lacan by the ego-psychologist Ernest Kris. A researcher had sought psychiatric help because he found himself in the grip of an uncontrollable urge to plagiarize. When the patient disclosed the name of the work he had recently plagiarized Kris was able to 'check it after the fact' (E 227/599). Kris discovered nothing untoward had transpired and concluded that his delusion was in fact a defence against actual plagiarism. Kris tried to assure his patient of this by confronting him with the evidence, only to have his patient reply that 'for some time, on leaving his sessions, he has wandered along a street full of attractive little restaurants, scrutinizing their menus in search of his favourite dish: fresh brains' (E 228/599).

This study clearly vindicates Kierkegaard's point: a direct attack on an illusion merely strengthens it. In this case the attack on the patient's illusion led the man to try literally, to digest another's brain! The study also graphically illustrates the strength of the fantasy or illusion with which analysis deals and the care needed in approaching it.

Kris's mistake was to assume the crude dichotomy of reality and fantasy – the methodological basis of modernity's critique of religion – believing that once the fantasy had been shown for what it is, a return to reality would ensue. However, as Lacan says: 'to side with the objective situation is going too far' (E 229/601). There can be no question of getting behind the fantasy; instead one must work with it. Indeed, to fail to take the fantasy seriously as Kris does, amounts to failing to take the question of desire seriously (E 229/602), i.e. it assumes reality can be rendered self-present to itself.

Intervention

One of the most distinguished tools of Lacanian analysis is the intervention. This took a number of forms: the repeated phrase, a protracted silence at the end of a statement, and most famously ending the session or *scansion*. The aim of intervention is to force the subject back onto his or her speech, so he or she might reflect on the import of what had just been said and its unconscious motivation.

Reading the works of Kierkegaard we are aware of the extent to which they preclude the type of conversation that constitutes analysis, but a conversation takes place nonetheless. We place ourselves before the texts and ask ourselves questions in the light thereof. In the front of *Stages on Life's Way*, a quote is taken from G. C. Lichtenberg: 'Such works are mirrors: when a monkey peers into them, no Apostle can be seen looking out'

(SLW 8). This passage exemplifies the role Kierkegaard ascribed to the pseudonymous works in undertaking the central dialectical role of analysis: reflecting back unconscious desires and motivations of the analysand.

Kierkegaard's pseudonyms offer a cultural analysis, mirroring back the personality types that we become. We recognize ourselves in the works and in turn they cause us not only to reflect on our lives, but also to make a decision about it. Indeed, in an analogy that seems to anticipate Lacan's insight into the unconscious and language, Kierkegaard describes the difference between the direct and indirect approaches in terms of the difference 'between writing on a blank piece of paper and bringing out by means of chemicals some writing that is hidden under other writing' (POV 54). The pseudonyms draw out and confront the motivations that lay hidden behind our actions. For example, as Amy Hall has argued, if we are in love, *Either/Or* confronts the degree to which our love is really the pursuit of self-interest (Hall, 2002, p. 2).

Intervention forces decision. In the 'Rome report', Lacan linked together three themes: intervention, the restructuring of the event after the fact [*nachträglich*] and '*the moment of concluding*' (E 48/257; italics in original). Intervention involves the analyst's interjections which illuminate the unconscious aspects of the analysand's speech. These offer a chance for the analysand to question how he has interpreted the defining events of his life. Through reinterpretation the subject is able to retroactively challenge the past after the event [*nachträglich*]. The point at which the analysand's past is decisively challenged by the analyst is the moment of concluding. The moment of concluding 'annuls the *time for understanding* in favour of the *moment of concluding* which precipitates the mediation of the subject towards deciding the meaning to attach to the original event' (E 48/257; italics in original). Taken together, intervention, the restructuring of the event after the fact [*nachträglich*] and the *moment of concluding*, bring about a crisis of decision in the subject concerning the signifiers that determine the meaning of his or her life.

The importance of this aspect of Lacanian analysis is much overlooked in favour of reading Lacan in terms of desire, where desire means the subject is given over to the lack that characterizes desire. However, while Lacan recognizes that selfhood is tied to loss, he does not preclude the centrality of agency; indeed Lacan advocates the role of decision in determining the narrative that constitutes selfhood because it is precisely by *not* making a decision that we are trapped by neurotic defences. Moreover, as we have seen, Kierkegaard voices the same anxiety over being's complicity in language and the loss entailed. So, despite Kierkegaard's claim that 'all decision is rooted in subjectivity', the decision itself opens up the 'wound of negativity' (CUP 85), which arises because 'The eternal decision that is sought is transformed into a continual striving' (CUP 2:47). In other words, for Kierkegaard no decision renders the subject finalized but takes account of the ceaseless task of becoming, a task he explicitly links to language: 'Only he really has style who is never finished with something but "stirs the waters of language" whenever he begins, so that to him the most ordinary expression comes into existence with newborn originality' (CUP 86). Kierkegaard's claim that we must immerse ourselves in the pool of language and risk the ceaseless task of becoming constitutes one way to describe the analytic process.

A Funny Thing Happened on the Way to the Clinic

When Lacan makes reference to Kierkegaard in his seminar 'The circuit' (SII 77–90) he identifies him as a 'humorist' (SII 87). The importance of this designation should not be overlooked. After all, why describe Kierkegaard as a humorist and not a Christian, melancholic, or Dane? Drawing on John Lippitt's provocative reading of humour in Kierkegaard's work, I suggest it is because Lacan saw the benefit of Kierkegaard's use of humour as an analytic tool.

Lacan often makes the association between analysis and humour. For example, he refers to 'the psychologist (not with-

out humour) and therapists (not without cunning)' (E 41/248)
and says:

> the closer we get to psychoanalysis being funny the more it is
> real psychoanalysis. Later on, it will get run in, it will be done
> by cutting corners and by pulling tricks. No one will under-
> stand any longer what's being done, just as there is no longer
> any need to understand anything about optics to make a
> microscope. (SI 77)

Furthermore, in his seminar on sexuality he delights in
Freud's name, *Freude* being the German for joy or pleasure:
'Freud, what a funny name – *Kraft durch Freud* [Strength
through joy], it's a whole platform! It is the funniest leap in the
sacred farce of history' (SXX 86).

But what precisely is the significance of humour? Freud
explored humour in *Jokes and their Relation to the Unconscious*
(1905). He argued that condensation and displacement, the
mechanisms of dream work, were to be found in the construction of jokes. In condensation a joke is created from a composite
word which compresses together a series of associations. For
example, the secondhand Sixties clothes shop in Bristol 'Re-
psycho' condenses 'recycle' with the title of an Alfred Hitchcock
film. Displacement involves diverting the reply from the
expected meaning of the reproach. For example, 'I was asked to
think of a large number, so I imagined a number one the size of
the Empire State building'. Here the numerical quality, 'large', is
displaced onto a physical quality, thereby diverting the expected
response. For Freud the pleasure of jokes relied on their ability
to lift inhibitions, either those of the enforced use of language,
or those of the subject matter. The semantic function of jokes
economizes on effort, and excess energy is liberated as laughter.
Jokes allow us to speak of troubling matters in a way that
deflects attention from our underlying neuroses while reminding
us of our pre-Oedipal joys:

> For the euphoria which we endeavour to reach by these
> means is nothing other than the mood of a period of life in

which we were accustomed to deal with our physical work in general with a small expenditure of energy – the mood of our childhood, when we were ignorant of the comic, when we were incapable of jokes and when we had no need of humour to make us feel happy in our life. (SE 8:236)

Lacan took *Jokes and their Relation to the Unconscious* (1905) as a seminal text because:

the effect of the unconscious is demonstrated in all its subtlety. And the visage it reveals to us is that of wit [*l'esprit*] in the ambiguity conferred on it by language . . . , in which its domination of reality [*réel*] is expressed in the challenge of non-meaning, and in which the humour, in the malicious grace of free spirit [*spirit libre*], symbolises a truth that does not say its last word. . . . It is truth, in fact, that throws off the mask in coming out of his mouth, but only so that the joke might take on another more deceptive mask. (E 59–60/270)

Lacan delights in jokes because they testify to the ambiguity of language, its ability to say one thing while meaning another, which in turn exemplifies the subject and the influence of the unconscious. However, Kierkegaard's use of humour in the *Postscript* throws open the door to another reading of Lacan's use of humour. Humour is one of the most striking aspects of *Postscript*. Its full title – *The Concluding Unscientific Postscript to 'Philosophical Fragments'* – parodies the title a speculative philosopher might use, setting up an internal contradiction between the pompousness of its title and its self-proclaimed status as *unscientific*; and although a postscript, the work is unusually four times longer than the book it follows.

Let us consider Climacus' view of humour. For Climacus, humour is rooted in contradiction: 'The comic is present in every stage of life . . . because where there is life there is contradiction, and wherever there is contradiction, the comic is present' (CUP 513–14). This theory is referred to as the incongruity theory: 'that the comic inheres in the relation of incongruity between two entities' (Lippitt, 2000, p. 8). To take one of Climacus' examples: 'Caricature is comic. By what means? By means of the contradiction between likeness and unlikeness.' If a caricature is too close it becomes portrait, and too far removed, it becomes 'meaningless fantasy' (CUP 517n.).

If one bears in mind the critique that author A made of Hegel in 'The immediate erotic stages' on the basis of language (the inner is incommensurable with the outer), it will become clear the value of humour's contradiction. As a force of contradiction, humour is the perfect vehicle for attacking Hegel's thesis because humour relies precisely on a contradiction which is not resolved.

Lippitt's study *Humour and Irony in Kierkegaard's Thought* provides a forceful argument in favour of the value of humour in the critique of Hegel. In particular he argues that 'Climacus aims to show speculative thought as *comical*, rather than simply mistaken', and the basis for this approach is the role humour plays as a 'vital form of indirect communication' (Lippitt, 2000, p. 5). Lippitt asks: If Hegel is wrong why not just say so? (Lippitt, 2000, p. 18). He provides a number of answers that touch on the issues we have dealt with in regard to indirect communication. I have organized them into four points.

First, to answer by simply expressing moral outrage misses the mark: one has nothing in common with the one being attacked. The aim is to change the other's outlook, not simply say that they are wrong. In this connection Lippitt makes the familiar point, that an illusion can never be destroyed directly; a direct attack only strengthens the person. By contrast, indirect communication involves a deception; it means not beginning directly, but by accepting the other's illusion as 'good money' (POV 53–4). Hegel's delusion is that he can occupy a position other than that of an existing human being, and *Postscript* parodies this position (Lippitt, 2000, p. 21). *Postscript* takes the form of the kind of dense philosophical text one expects from Hegel, and it is likely to be read by the type of person who would read Hegel; yet it forces that thinker to think about the content of his illusion. Gradually the contradiction between Hegel's system and his position as an existing individual dawns;

we see the humour of our own position. Second, any direct criticism can be accommodated by tweaking the system and thus be taken up into the system rather than challenging it (Lippitt, 2000, p. 22). Third, laughter can 'liberate us from the sense of feeling obliged to argue against the system on its own terms' (Lippitt, 2000, p. 22). This point is also made by Hermann Cloeren who refers to laughter's 'therapeutic effect' (Cloeren, 1985, p. 4). Laughter 'terminates anxiety caused by not understanding Hegel' and dispels 'the worries of being unable to solve the problems of speculative philosophy' (Lippitt, 2000, p. 4). Fourth, humour has a function of humility (Lippitt, 2000, p. 59), an argument also made by C. Stephen Evans. Humour is a protection against pride because in refusing a direct moralizing critique one 'does not wish to appear outwardly better than other men' (Evans, 1983, p. 205).

Taken together these points throw valuable light on the pedagogic function of humour in Lacanian analysis. As Lacan says: 'excursions into the ridiculous must be used for their eye-opening value, since by opening our eyes to the absurdity of a theory, they direct our attention back to dangers that have nothing theoretical about them' (E 53/263). The use of jokes and humour proves a valuable corrective against over-theorizing the analytic experience as Hegel did of Christianity. Humour also confers the spirit of contradiction on the session, which challenges the unity perceived by the imaginary order.

Consider also Mario Beira's example. An analysand who was sexually shy said he was going abroad to Amsterdam. Beira's reply 'have fun' teased out a pun on the word 'a broad' (Beira, 2000, p. 183). Was the subject going abroad – to a different country, or was he going to find 'a broad', 'a broad' being the American slang for a prostitute? The joke relies on displacement, creating a comic contrast between a holiday and a whore. Like Kierkegaard's parodies of Hegel, the joke is subtle enough to avoid being a direct statement which may appear judgemental; instead it lends itself to further interpretation making the subject active in that interpretation. Furthermore, in refusing to offer a clear judgement upon the analysand, the analyst is not elevating himself above the analysand, but maintains his humility.

Psychoanalysis, Analogy, and Participation

In *Postscript* Climacus' discussion of subjectivity leads him to draw a comparison between his own indirect method and God's relation to creation:

> Oddly enough, although there is so much clamouring for the positive and for the direct communication of results, it does not occur to anyone to complain about God . . . No anonymous author can more slyly hide himself, and no maieutic can more carefully recede from a direct relation than God can. He is in the creation, everywhere in the creation, but he is not there directly . . . Nature is certainly the work of God, but only the work is directly present, not God. (CUP 243)

This passage is important for my argument because it clearly shows that Kierkegaard viewed his own relation to the pseudonymous authorship in terms of God's relation to the world: God is compared to the anonymous author. In both cases the distance between the creator and created is productive in terms of procuring subjective reflection: Kierkegaard's indirect method repeats God's indirect relation to the world in that it aims to both establish and protect the freedom of the subject in his or her appropriation of truth.

Shakespeare argues that the relation between the two is analogical in the Thomist sense of the word (Shakespeare, 2001, pp. 180–6).[1] Aquinas famously argued in the *Summa Contra Gentiles* that: 'Effects that fall short of their causes do not agree with them in name and nature. Yet, some likeness must be found between them, since it belongs to the nature of action

---

1 C. Fabro has argued that Aquinas' doctrine of analogy is the 'basis of his [Kierkegaard's] entire thinking' (Fabro, 1980, p. 97).

that an agent produces its like' (*SCG* I. 29, 2). That is to say, the form of the effect (e.g. heat) will be found to a degree in the cause (e.g. fire). Aquinas argues that the nature of that participation is best described as analogical. If causality were univocal such that one could predicate univocal terms then 'an effect should measure up to the species of its cause' (*SCG* I. 32, 3). With regard to God and man this would amount to humans possessing the same divine perfections. If predication is equivocal then 'there is no likeness in things themselves; there is only the unity of name' (*SCG* I. 33, 2). That is to say, we cannot talk meaningfully about God and our relation to him. However, Aquinas says we can speak of our relation analogically (*SCG* I. 34). Speaking analogously implies a similarity within a greater difference, it allows for a likeness that in no way infringes upon God's transcendence, yet nor does it plunge one into silence.

Shakespeare situates the relationship between Kierkegaard's indirect communication and Aquinas' analogy overwhelmingly within the critical and apophatic sense: clarifying what cannot be said of God rather than what can, thereby curtailing the idolatry of direct relations with God. For Shakespeare, to speak of God as the indirect author is primarily to render God 'wholly other' (Shakespeare, 2001, p. 220). However, he makes what is arguably a far more salient comment in his approach to Kierkegaard, indirect communication, and analogy, which I expand upon within the context of psychoanalysis: given the analogy between God's communication and indirect communication, it is possible to suggest that the latter involves us as 'co-workers in the creative work of God' (Shakespeare, 2001, p. 195). The point made here is that if God creates indirectly, then to practise maieutics becomes itself a form of analogical participation in God's causality. In order to understand this, let us recall first, what is implied in maieutics. In creation God is in nature, yet not directly present. This sentiment is also expressed through Kierkegaard's figurative description of revelation in *Fragments*: a king falls in love with a maiden, and adopts the position of a lowly servant to ensure that she, in her freedom, comes to love him (PF 26–31). God is present as the servant

Christ, yet indirectly so. Climacus links this to the method of indirect communication associated with Socrates (PF 30). This figurative analogy is crucial because it highlights that the form of communication is both motivated by love, and tries to cultivate a freely loving response. Kierkegaard reinforces the relation between maieutics and love in *Works of Love* where he says:

> in the world of spirit . . . to become one's own master is the highest – and in love to help someone toward that, to become himself, free, independent, his own master, to help him stand alone – that is the greatest beneficence. (WL 274)

From the foregoing discussion two aspects emerge: first, God creates a realm of freedom, a realm of created independence; second, God creates this realm out of love. Put together, it is possible to say that we participate in God inasmuch as we practise maieutic causality, motivated by love to create the conditions of freedom that allow the subject to subsequently direct oneself and others towards God. In this way, analytic causality becomes analogical to God's causality.

This approach helps to focus just what is at stake in the analogy of being and refine the doctrine of participation. As Conor Cunningham has put it with regard to the analogy of being, it is not simply that we can analogically refer our being (*esse*) back to God. Rather, it is the case that *being* is analogical: we are like God only inasmuch as we participate in divine causality, through causing things in an analogical manner, that is, creating realms of independence (Cunningham, 2002, p. 184).

I both strengthen this contention and deepen the analysis by referring to the work of Milbank and Pickstock on Aquinas. They have stressed that for Aquinas, God creates with his intellect not just his nature. Like Cunningham, they stress that what is at stake in our relation to God is not that we simply share being, which is to say that our analogical participation is founded upon *esse*, but that we share intellect also: *esse intelligible* (Milbank and Pickstock, 2001, p. 8). Everything depends here on what is meant by intellect. Intellect is not 'indifferent speculation; it is rather a beautiful ratio which is instantiated between things and the mind' (Milbank and Pickstock, 2001, p. 9). That is to say, intellect is an aesthetic judgement tied to the ability to discern truth, where truth is how a thing conforms to the integrity of its being. As Catherine Pickstock says, 'One might begin by saying that truth is a property of things, that a thing is true if it fulfils itself and holds itself together according to its character and goal' (Milbank and Pickstock, 2001, p. 9). That is to say, if a thing realizes itself in its *telos*.[2] So for example, rain fulfils its *telos* when it is being rainy (Milbank and Pickstock, 2001, p. 10). In fulfilling its *telos* it copies the mind of God, analogically participating in him. As Aquinas says, 'A craftsman is said to produce a false work if it falls short of the proper operation of his art.' (*ST* I, q. 17, a. 1, resp.). It is important to recognize that for both Milbank and Pickstock, analogy and participation find expression in the central role given to liturgy, doxology, and the Eucharist (Milbank and Pickstock, 2001, pp. 341–52). Indeed, the liturgy is central to analogy because it provides the interpretive framework that allows analogy and participation to work at all because liturgy provides the discursive rules by which we can refer ourselves back to the creator.

I suggest that Kierkegaard also invites this participatory quality in doxology, such that the task of fulfilling one's *telos* means giving worship to God because '*Worship* is the maximum for a human being's relation to God' (CUP 413; italics in original). Expanding this out into the context of the work of analysis, one can say that the analyst is a craftsman who, like God, creates realms of independence that open out into worship, the *telos* (maximum) of creation. In this sense Kierkegaard's indirect communication, or rather, Lacanian analysis

---

2 In this respect she quotes *ST* I, q. 16, a. 1, resp. 'Natural things are said to be true in so far as they express the likeness of the species that are in the divine mind. For a stone is called true, which possesses the nature proper to a stone, according to the preconception in the divine intellect' (Milbank and Pickstock, 2001, p. 114, n. 34).

repeated through Kierkegaard, becomes a form of analogical participation in God's creative causality because to participate in God as cause not only means one refers back to the prime cause recognizing a certain likeness, it is also to practise creative causality itself, to create in an intelligent way, to encourage others in their assumption of desire with worship as its end.

Situating analysis in this way helps it to become a work of love in a way that Lacanian analysis cannot be,[3] a criticism Kierkegaard had already anticipated. In *Works of Love* Kierkegaard differentiates between Socratic and Christian maieutics in terms of neighbourly love. The secular maieutic teacher helps someone to stand on their own, but retains a satisfaction that the other stands on his own – 'through another's help' (WL 275). By contrast, the Christian maieutic teacher, '*giving thanks to God*, he declares: Now this individual is standing by himself – through my help. But there is no self-satisfaction in the last phrase' (WL 278; italics mine). For the Christian, helping others testifies to God's sustaining love. Contrast this with Lacan. In his Seminar *Transference*, the analyst is compared to the figure of Socrates in Plato's *Symposium*, a figure in the service of Eros. The comparison forms the basis for arguing that transference is established through love. However, for Lacan the basis for stimulating transferential love is the Greek *agalma* – a statue offered to the gods and hidden in a worthless box – which is none other than the *objet petit a*: love is stimulated by the signifier of our incompleteness, but this remains a purely structural definition at the level of signification, and the aim of

---

3 Julia Kristeva, a pupil of Lacan's, has already argued that Lacanian analysis is unable to practise love. In particular she is critical of the father function. She questions why any child should make the transition to the symbolic if the paternal function operates purely on the basis of negative threats. She argues that the imaginary father also includes a loving trusting aspect, supporting the child in her transition (Kristeva, 1997, p. 132). However, it is questionable whether the father function for Lacan is as negative as she suggests because the father function frees the subject from the anxiety of trying to be the illusive phallus for the mother, an impossible task (SV 22.1.58).

analysis is to expose that signifier for what it is (SVIII 177). Moreover, Lacan had already dealt with 'love of one's neighbour' the year before. Here he offers little advance on Freud for whom the ideality of the commandment to love 'is justified by the fact that nothing else runs so strongly counter to the original nature of man' (SE 21:112). Lacan simply highlights and condenses, on the basis of Freud, the figure of love and its counter-nature into *jouissance*, arguing that all pleasure is fundamentally linked to 'evil' (SVII 186). In this way Lacan echoes Freud's sentiment that the subject is always caught between the antithesis of love and discord, *Eros* and *Thanatos* (SE 23:244–7).

Kristeva has made a similar claim regarding Lacan, psychoanalysis, love and theology. Her approach centres upon the trust and faith that the analysand must have for the analyst, and the analyst's desire to help. She subverts Freud's claim that psychoanalysis has its own God: *Logos* (SE 21:54), reinterpreting it in the light of John 1.1 and 1 John 4.8: 'In the beginning was the Word', and 'God is love'. By situating love in terms of God's creative expression, she is closer to Kierkegaard than Lacan. However, as long as she employs theological terms for purely strategic matters rather than as an affirmation of theological practice, her use of theology remains pragmatic (Kristeva, 1987, p. 3).

In summary, for Lacan analytic love is a function of the signifier, and one part of an irreducible conflict. For Kierkegaard love becomes an opening into transcendence. The relationship between God's indirect method and Kierkegaard's indirect communication tentatively points in the direction of envisaging God as what I call the 'arch-analyst', the principal analyst whose love for man leads him to fashion an indirect yet incisive intervention into time through the work of Christ. This helps to establish an analogical relationship flowing from God to man's analytic practice. Analytic intervention is similar to, albeit different from, God's intervention. In the following chapters I ground that analogical relation in the liturgy of the Eucharist.

6

Time for Analysis

Introduction

A central requirement of analysis is that the analysand appropriates time existentially because analysis is not a question of learning to live in an eternal present, but precisely the opposite: taking one's history seriously, where one has come from, where one is, and where one is going. In this regard Lacan makes explicit reference to Heidegger, for whom an existential approach is stimulated by a dramatic encounter with one's mortality. This dramatic encounter becomes the model of the analytic intervention which forces subjects to take their own history seriously. However, as I argue, Heidegger's approach is in turn indebted to Kierkegaard, for whom time only arises in the context of the Incarnation, God's dramatic intervention into the world. This leads me to the remarkable conclusion that Christ's traumatic intervention is the paradigm for the analytic intervention, and hence analysis is a theological parody. By exposing the theological borrowings of analysis, I lay the ground in this chapter for the following, where I argue that Christ's repeated intervention in the Sacred Mass may be seen in terms of analytic intervention, and hence the Sacred Mass may be seen in terms of a social form of analysis.

An Anxious Time

One of the major problems faced by analysands is the power their neurotic defences exercise over them, thwarting the attempt to realize thought in action. For example, it may be the case that a woman wants a relationship where she is respected for who she is, yet a neurotic disposition causes her to enter relations where she ends up conforming to the man's desire (the position of the hysteric) in order to justify her worth. In this instance analysis involves breaking out of the defences that structure neurotic *jouissance*. This principally entails challenging the assumption that the past is irretrievably behind us. Central to this process is learning to understand the signifiers that structure one's neurosis, and this involves what Lacan terms *anamnesis*: remembering past events. But this is not undertaken in terms of the factual recounting of events and their chain of causality as if an accurate representation of reality will suddenly dispel the neurosis. Such an approach overlooks the nature of language within which the past takes place. For this reason Lacan characterizes the process using an explicit reference to Heidegger's use of the grammatical tense: future anterior; the implication being that the past is always open to the retroactive nature of meaning, because how one determines the present affects how one understands the past.

Heidegger's analysis of *Dasein* poses the question: 'does not anxiety get constituted by a future? Certainly; but not by the inauthentic future of awaiting' (Heidegger, 1962, p. 393). We are not simply anxious about what the future holds, rather:

> anxiety brings one back to one's throwness as something *possible* which *can be repeated*. And in this way it *also* reveals the possibility of an authentic potentiality-for-Being – a potentiality which must, in repeating, come back to its thrown 'there', but come back as something future which comes towards [*zukünftiges*]. (Heidegger, 1962, p. 393)

In this dense passage Heidegger makes the point that anxiety about the future bears down upon us to reveal the way we have been situated, the way we are already begun, part of a community, constituted by our heritage. In turn our heritage discloses future possibilities for the repetition thereof. For example: if my father was a carpenter it would be part of my cultural heritage, it is not outside of my frame of reference to become a carpenter, it thereby becomes a possibility that I may choose to repeat, actualizing it in the present. However, notice the temporal paradox: should I become a carpenter then I would repeat the past on the basis of it coming towards me from the future; I could discover my potential coming back to me (*zukünftiges*) from the future.

Heidegger calls this point of intersection in which the past is illuminated by the future coming towards us in the present '*Augenblick*', which translates as 'the moment of vision' or 'the glance of an eye' (Heidegger, 1962, p. 387). *Augenblick* is the point at which we encounter how things look differently in the light of the future possibilities, revealing the potentiality of our past.

That Heidegger roots anxiety and being in history is not lost on Lacan. Indeed, given Lacan's thesis that the subject emerges in the field of the Other, Lacanian analysis in no way avoids the determinative elements of our past. Although analysis aims to reconfigure the past on the basis of the future this is not a licence to invent a life one never had with a view to changing the past, precisely because we always are already begun. In analysis the subject 'relates in the present the origins of her person' (E 47/255). However, the subject can learn to see the different potential for signification that past events are open to, she must recognize the ambiguity of all significations and make a decision about how events return to them from the future; the analysand must choose a different past to return to in the future, 'reorder[ing] past contingencies by conferring on them the sense of necessities to come' (E 48/256). The subject becomes creative with her past in a way that presupposes the narrative that formed her. Through the decisions the subject makes about past signification, new perspectives open up which coterminously restructure the past, retroactively reconfiguring it and hence releasing the subject for action in the present.

Time for Kierkegaard

In all of this, the figure of Kierkegaard should not be lost because his account of repetition anticipates this temporal loop. Consider first the aim of the analytic intervention: to open up a space where one may repeat the past but on the basis of a difference, that is, without the neurosis. Is this not the structure of repetition? Second, both repetition and analysis require full existential commitment to action in the present; and third, repetition and analysis are both transcendent inasmuch as they demand a change in the subject. In order to strengthen this central contention I want to look at Kierkegaard's discussion of time.

In *The Concept of Anxiety* (1844) the pseudonym Vigilius Haufniensis outlines two concepts of time that correspond to recollection and repetition: Greek/pagan consciousness of time and a specifically Christian consciousness of time (CA 85–91). In both cases the definition of time as 'the succession that passes by' (CA 86) holds. The difference belongs to the way time is divided into its past, present, and future, and the relative position of eternity.

Greek time

Haufniensis argues that Greek/pagan time is tied to a spatial understanding. This proves incongruous with time as an infinite succession when it comes to speaking about the past, present, and future because a spatial concept of time undermines those very tenses. Crucially for Kierkegaard this preclusion denies any sense of developing selfhood. Let us follow his argument in more detail. Kierkegaard says that for the Greeks, time and space are identical (CA 85). That is to say, the Greeks' view of time is conceptualized around the movement of an object through space. Mark C. Taylor usefully exemplifies Aristotle's account in his study of Kierkegaard and time (Taylor, 1975, pp. 82–5). According to Aristotle, time is a means by which the motion of objects through space can be measured (*Physics*, IV, 219a–222a). For example, Aristotle writes, 'for it is by means of the body that is carried along that we become aware of the "before and after" in the motion' (*Physics*, IV, 11, 219b). Time is subordinated to the object that moves. As the object follows its course through space the area already travelled becomes the past, the area yet to be travelled is the future, while the space occupied by the object is the present (Taylor, 1975, p. 83).

The problem arises however because the distinction between the past, present, and future is implicit to time itself; they are divisions along an imagined line. However, because the line is a constant succession, no present dividing line can ever gain a real 'foothold' (CA 85). As soon as you introduce a line into the succession discriminating the tenses it appears behind you in the past. And because no moment can be present, 'accordingly there is in time neither present, nor past, nor future' (CA 85). In Greek/pagan time the present is only ever an abstract line drawn to divide, yet in the same moment it moves into the past because of the constant succession of time, and therefore it ceases to be the present. This makes the present infinitely vanishing, thus the life that is only construed in terms of belief 'in time' (CA 86) has no present. It will be recalled that this was how Heidegger characterized inauthentic time, as a succession of 'nows' (Heidegger, 1962, p. 474).

Just as the divisions in Greek/pagan time are implicit to time, so the Greek/pagan concept of the eternal is immanent to time. In this model eternity is simply the infinite succession, defined in either a backward or forward direction, although Kierkegaard argues that given the Greek doctrine of recollection, eternity is usually equated with a backward motion (R 131). So, for the Greeks there is no qualitative difference between time and eternity, eternity is simply time under the aspect of infinity, and for this reason it lends itself to the doctrine of recollection. The doctrine of recollection does not require that the subject be given some extra truth from outside, rather truth is contained within. In this way the doctrine of recollection can be said to shore up the realm of immanence by both denying a qualitative change in the subject (they discover what they already knew), as well as denying any qualitative difference between eternity and time.

Christian time

By contrast, Christian consciousness of time is fashioned by the claim that the eternal entered time. And herein lies the distinctiveness of the Christian approach which underpins repetition: in Christianity the eternal is taken as qualitatively different from time; the eternal *enters* time rather than describes a property *of* time. And because the eternal is qualitatively different from time and yet enters time, it decisively annuls time's infinite 'succession' (CA 86). Thus from the perspective of Kierkegaard's consciousness of time, the eternal is not immanent to time in terms of the entirety of its succession, but transcendent in terms of its decisive annulment of time. It is precisely the annulment of time at its intersection with eternity that creates the stable foothold needed for the present. The intersection of time and eternity in the present is not simply an abstract point of division, immanent and hence swept back up into the succession, but a decisive break which ensures a genuine foothold. Kierkegaard calls this decisive break, 'the instant' or 'moment' (*Øiblikket*, 'a blink of the eye'):

> The moment is that ambiguity in which time and eternity touch each other, and with this the concept of *temporality* is posited, whereby time constantly intersects eternity and eternity constantly pervades time. As a result, the above-mentioned division acquires its significance: the present time, the past time, and the future time. (CA 89)

As Louis Dupré says, 'Far from abolishing history, the instant gives it an unprecedented importance: the moment of objective presence of the eternal in time divides history into A.D. and B.C.' (Dupré, 1985, p. 128). However, as Haufniensis suggests, eternity's intersection with time is not a singular event, rather, 'eternity constantly pervades time' (CA 89).

Now the philosopher may rightly wish to argue that Kierkegaard has not really implied any real alternative because, after all, it is not as if a stable point outside of time by which to measure the succession has been found; one is still relating to a point inside time. Indeed, Christians seem to make a virtue of this: God became man and dwelt among us. The Christian faith, excluding its humanist forms, believes in the historical presence of God on earth. Therefore what is to stop the eternal being swept up into the infinite succession, why should the Greek consciousness of time be any different from the Christian consciousness?

But such a response misses Kierkegaard's argument. Because the eternal is taken by Kierkegaard to be qualitatively different from the temporal, its place within time is never one that is fully integrated – it is a point of *trauma*. Such a reading would concur with Kierkegaard's critique of Hegel, that there can be no final synthesis in the dialectic. For Kierkegaard there is no harmonious whole, life is a series of conflicting oppositions that resist all mediation. And this is the crucial point, the Christian understanding of the temporal succession includes a traumatic element that cannot be fully assimilated, and it is this recognition that brings the tenses into relief because it shifts the apprehension of time from an objective problem to a subjective phenomenon. In other words, a point of trauma is constitutive of the subjective approach because it prevents one from transcending oneself in the hope of objective knowledge. Consider for example Aristotle's argument. For him to view time spatially he must implicitly occupy a transcendental position from which he can objectively look down upon it, a neutral point by which he can measure the succession. And because he is now divorced from time, his account lacks any existential concern, the anxiety of the future or regret of the past. Moreover, when this same Aristotelian approach is adopted by John McTaggart, it leads McTaggart to deny the reality of time altogether (McTaggart, 2001, pp. 260–71), thus confirming Kierkegaard's point that viewed objectively time disappears (CA 85).[1]

---

1 For a more detailed engagement between Kierkegaard and McTaggart see 'Having a good time with Kierkegaard: McTaggart, Kierkegaard, and the ethical status of time' (Pound, 2005, pp. 13–22).

The relation between the eternal and the temporal can be further conceptualized with the aid of Žižek's critical comments on Schelling whose lectures had been attended by Kierkegaard during the winter of 1842 (Žižek, 2000a, pp. 92–107). Žižek argues that in Schelling's work, the relation between time and eternity is comparable to the relation between an event and its structure, where the event that gives rise to a structure is subsequently repressed. Henceforth the event exists as an unassailable trauma; in Lacanian terms this is the relation between the real and the symbolic: the real is that which is given up as condition of entry into the symbolic and subsequently known only negatively as an unassailable trauma (Žižek, 2000a, p. 96). Likewise, the eternal is the event (the real) that gives rise to history (the symbolic). Eternity allows historical reality to maintain its consistency but only by refusing to be fully integrated, which is Kierkegaard's point precisely: eternity 'intersects' time creating the tensed order, however, within time it is a disruptive force, it is not integrated into time. Only in Greek time is the eternal integrated, eternity being time in its entirety (CA 89).

This traumatic kernel is exemplified by the decrees of the Chalcedonian Council (451) on Christ, intended as they were to clarify doctrine in the light of Monophysitic and Nestorian heresies. The Monophysitic heresy declared that Christ had but a single and divine nature (οὐσια) thus resolving the temporal into the eternal (a Gnostic heresy). The Nestorian heresy declared that Christ was two persons (πρόσωπον), one human and the other divine, and that these two did not commingle. Nestorians referred to a conjunction/connexion (συνάφεια) rather than a union (ἕνωσις), denying to Mary the title theotokos (θεοτόκος). They considered her as mother only of the human person of Christ. In contrast, the Council of Chalcedon affirmed the existence of one person in two natures, 'united unconfusedly, unchangeably, indivisibly, inseparably' (Cross, 1957, p. 916). Christ is neither two separate persons (Nestorian), nor are those two resolved into a single nature (Monophysitic): Christ is one person whose wholly divine (eternal) nature is the exception that grounds his whole humanity (temporality).

Moreover, any attempt to resolve the problematic kernel of the Incarnation by positing a definitive break or resolving the two into one, amounts to a neurotic defence, an avoidance of the antagonist kernel that constitutes his being. In psychoanalytic and theological terms this implies that any heretical move (and that includes humanism) to resolve the problematic relation of the eternal and temporal amounts to an avoidance of the traumatic kernel which is unsound not only doctrinally but psychologically too.

Kierkegaard also provides an argument here far in advance of the claims of postmodernists like Mark C. Taylor who argue that only with the death or loss of the transcendental signifier does the realm of the temporal truly open up (Taylor, 1984, p. 14). Only when the temporal is related to its other, the eternal, can a genuine sense of temporality open up. Hence Kierkegaard accused the Greeks of not having a concept of the eternal in 'a deeper sense', by which he means as a category distinct from time; and while they privileged the past in terms of the doctrine of recollection, the past posited by recollection was not a past time defined in relation to the present and the future but 'a qualification of time in general' (CA 89).

The instant [*Øiblikket*] introduces the tenses into the succession of time by decisively annulling that succession. Haufniensis also talks about this point in terms of 'the fullness of time', a phrase taken from Galatians 4.4 (CA 246 n. 27). What is at stake in the fullness of time is not simply the moment as the division of time into the tenses, but the point where the eternal, in the present, draws together the tenses, bridging the past and future. The theological root of this expression should qualify this aspect further: in the fullness of time future hope redeems the past.

The pivotal concept in Christianity, that which makes all things new, is the fullness of time, but the fullness of time is the moment as the eternal, and yet this eternal is also the future and the past. If attention is not paid to this, not a single concept can be saved from a heretical and treasonable admixture that annihilates the concept. One does not get the past by itself but in a simple continuity with the future (with this the concepts of conversion, atonement, and redemption are lost in the world-historical significance and lost in the individual historical development). The future is not by itself but in a simple continuity with the present (thereby the concepts of resurrection and judgement are destroyed). (CA 90)

Haufniensis' exposition of time places great store in the future. The future's privileged status arises because 'the future can in a certain sense signify the whole' (CA 89) but also because of its relation to anxiety:

> For freedom, the possible is the future, and the future is for time the possible. To both of these corresponds anxiety in the individual life. An accurate and correct linguistic usage therefore associates anxiety and the future. When it is sometimes said that one is anxious about the past, this seems to be a contradiction of the usage. . . . If I am anxious about a past misfortune, then this is not because it is in the past but because it may be repeated, i.e., become future. (CA 91)

Haufniensis' point is that the moment introduces anxiety because through its annulment of time's succession the future comes into view, bearing down upon the subject in terms of the possibilities to which life is open. As he says: '[A]nxiety is the moment' (CA 81), because anxiety is 'freedom's possibility' (CA 155) and demands we make a choice about our lives.

Repetition/*Augenblick*

Given the above it is possible to discern the influence Kierkegaard had on Heidegger and by extension Lacan. First, it was Kierkegaard who initially articulated how anxiety about the future was tied to the way the past comes towards us from the future (CA 91). Second, one should note the influence that Kierkegaard's category of the instant [*Øiblikket*] has on

Heidegger's term *Augenblick*. *Augenblick* or 'the moment of vision' is clearly related to *Øiblikket*, figuratively derived from *Øiets blik*, a blink of the eye (Heidegger, 1962, p. 387; Magurshak, 1985, pp. 167–95). What is at stake in both *Øiblikket* and *Augenblick* is the point of intersection between the past, present, and future, and the concerned engagement the subject brings to that temporal structure. For Heidegger the moment is the opening for the nostalgic retrieval of the potentiality for Being. For Lacan it becomes the point at which the subject breaks out of neurosis by repeating the past with a difference; and for Kierkegaard it becomes repetition in the highest sense of the word: atonement, in which we win ourselves back in the light of God.

Third, Kierkegaard shows how it was only with the event of the Incarnation that this consciousness of time arose, because only when the eternal enters time is there the decisive annulment of time, such that the tenses are established. Only with the Incarnation is temporality posited; and only in the Incarnation are those same tenses given 'simple continuity' (CA 90): the past redeems the present by arriving in the form of hope from the future.

I would therefore suggest that the decisive intervention the analyst seeks to establish is a parody of Christ's intervention. The analyst's intervention seeks to manifest the trauma of the real through disrupting the imaginary axis and thereby bring temporality into view. However, unlike Christianity, for Lacan one need not rely on an external agent to puncture the imaginary. Certainly, by virtue of their training, analysts are in a special position to do so; nonetheless there are enough immanently established points to unsettle the specular image of unity. For example, in 'The subversion of the subject and the dialectic of desire', Lacan suggests that the image of the genital region 'concentrating in itself the most intimate aspect of autoeroticism' (E 307/822) upsets the imaginary image. Moreover, the gap between the specular image of oneself and one's empirical experience of motor coordination will generate a frustration that unsettles the imaginary dream of wholeness. Hence one can situate Lacanian analysis within what Kierkegaard calls 'religiousness *A*' – inasmuch as it encourages a subjective appropriation of truth without requiring that the subject relate to the eternal in such a way as to constitute subjectivity as untruth (that is, sin). Indeed, as I have shown, for Lacan sin is simply transcribed in terms of an 'Other'. Only when the subject's point of departure relies on the historically contingent evidence of Christ entering time and telling us we are in sin is religiousness *B* properly constituted, the properly paradoxical religion (CUP 556). However, as I will argue in the next chapter, when analysis constitutes itself in terms of 'religiousness *B*', it ceases to become analysis and becomes eucharistic devotion. This is not to preclude analysis, but set it within an ecclesial framework.

Conclusion

If my analysis is correct, it should be clear that it is only subsequent to the Incarnation that there can be analysis at all. This is not an obvious claim that simply gives testimony to two thousand years of formative history in-between, but a reference to the qualitative shift in consciousness that Christianity invites and is historically mediated to Lacan from Kierkegaard, through Heidegger.

One of the questions raised by this claim is: if Christ's intervention is paradigmatic of the analytic intervention, to what extent can Christ's repeated intervention in the Liturgy of the Eucharist be seen in terms of analytic categories? Said otherwise, is there a case to be made that the Eucharist repeats Christ's intervention and thereby constitutes a social form of analysis? I shall explore this question in the next and final chapter. In doing so I argue that the Eucharist does perform such an intervention which helps the communicant assume his or her desire. The communicant's encounter with the Christ-Word brings the subject to full speech as well as embedding analytic practice within a wider social praxis.

7

Towards a Liturgical Therapeutics

Introduction

In the previous chapters I have shown the degree to which Kierkegaard's aims and methods are commensurate with Lacanian analysis inasmuch as both employ an indirect approach to the subject aimed at cultivating the subjective appropriation of truth which, I have argued, can also be expressed as the assumption of desire. Particular attention was given to the model of time outlined in Heidegger and Lacan's work on the basis of Kierkegaard's distinction between the Christian and Greek/pagan consciousness of time. I have argued that Christ's intervention into time serves as the paradigm for all subsequent analytic interventions. In pagan time the subject is left at the mercy of the instant and hence a slave to his own impulses. When analysis adopts this mode of time it can do no more than advise patients to follow their instinct or metaphorically to follow their heart – the new-age equivalent of the Platonic doctrine of recollection. But Christian time construes the eternal as qualitatively different from time, and as such a traumatic incursion *in* time. This traumatic break brings the tenses into relief, and subsequently allows one to situate oneself with regard to the past as well as future possibilities. Analysis adopts this mode of time in its use of the intervention and restructuring of the past with a view to breaking out of neuroses.

In this chapter I extend the relation between Kierkegaard's aims and methods and Lacanian analysis in the light of the Eucharist, as observed in the Sacred Mass. My reasons for doing so are threefold: first, this chapter marks a logical step from the previous chapter where Christ's dual nature was defended in both analytic and theological terms. Catholic doctrine affirms that the Eucharist *is* Christ, and hence what I have said about Christ can be said about the Eucharist. Second, thinking about the Eucharist in Kierkegaardian and Lacanian terms is a means to take their work into new territory. Third, by considering Lacan and Kierkegaard in the light of the Eucharist I provide an ecclesial setting to my work.

This last point is crucial, because just as Lacan's work is rooted in clinical practice so too the Church's work is rooted in liturgical practice. Thus, only by situating Lacan and Kierkegaard in liturgical practice can one achieve praxis: the unity of thought and action. Moreover, as I argue, the liturgical setting ensures against psychoanalysis becoming a mere 'emptying of oneself into nothingness' (Ward, 2000, p. 108), being instead the practice of love, part of the redemptive process of creation.

My argument in this chapter is simple even if my sources are unorthodox. I adopt a Protestant (Kierkegaard) and an atheist (Lacan) to defend the Catholic doctrine of the Eucharist and its institution. I argue that the liturgy of the Eucharist is analogous to analysis inasmuch as it helps to procure subjective reflection upon the truth: the assumption of desire; although ultimately I argue that it surpasses Lacanian analysis because whereas Lacan consigns the subject to a despairing lack, eucharistic devotion points the subject towards the divine plenitude of God's love.

Given that I am defending a Catholic view of the Eucharist, yet employing a Protestant to do so, I begin by examining Kierkegaard's attitudes to the sacrament. Next I consider the relation between Christ and the Eucharist. I then move on to compare the Eucharist and its practice with the themes of analysis developed in the previous chapter. I end by articulating the difference that eucharistic intervention adds to a purely secular understanding of the analytic intervention.

Kierkegaard and Sacrament

Given Kierkegaard's emphasis on the subjective life of the Christian, one might readily assume he would maintain a basic distrust of the sacraments as external signs. Indeed, in one journal entry he applauds Pascal's critique that 'Christianity with the help of some sacraments excuses itself from loving God' (JP 1:543). And later on he says: '[T]he church is made into a communion of indifferent existences (or where the existential is a matter of indifference) – but the 'doctrine' is correct and the sacraments are rightly administered. This is really paganism' (JP 1:600). This is certainly the conclusion Louis Dupré arrives at: 'It should be obvious that sacraments in the Catholic, or even in the orthodox Lutheran, sense of the word are incompatible with Kierkegaard's theory' (Dupré, 1963, p. 106). Moreover, one could strengthen Dupré's contention by pointing to Kierkegaard's rejection of Luther's doctrine of ubiquity: 'People . . . have developed a doctrine of the ubiquity of Christ's body, and with that they have in Christendom a fantastic notion of Christ' (TC 101). It is likely that Kierkegaard's contention here was not Luther's *communicatio idiomatum* regarding the ubiquitarian debate, but the need to underwrite the sacrament of the Eucharist with the real presence of Christ.[1] After all, Kierkegaard was not given to the arguments of the scholastic writers, and would later refer to the Eucharist simply as a 'token of the reception of the Lord'.[2]

Yet arguably, Kierkegaard's polemics against the sacraments implies the obverse: he took the sacraments *absolutely serious-*

---

1 Luther was one of the few reformers to maintain the doctrine of the real presence of Christ in the Eucharist. The doctrine of ubiquity to which he also held suggested that Christ in his human nature is everywhere present. However, this was considered an incorrect application of divine predicates to the human aspect of Christ (*communicatio idiomatum*), thereby fudging the distinction between the two natures (Maas, 1912, p. 169).

2 Kierkegaard, *Edifying Discourses* (Augsburg Publishing House, 1950), quoted in Dupré, 1963, p. 106 n. 36.

ly. Kierkegaard's point is not that one should dispense with the sacraments, but that one should be existentially committed to them. Consider for example his critique of the reformer Ulrich Zwingli (1484–1531) for whom the Eucharist was just a symbolic act of remembrance:

> the Lord's Supper is called Communion with Him; it is not merely in remembrance of Him, not merely a pledge that thou hast communion with Him, but it is the communion, the communion which thou shalt endeavour to maintain in thy daily life by more and more living thyself out of thyself and living thyself into Him, into His love. (FSE 24–5)

The danger for Kierkegaard occurs when one objectifies the Eucharist at the expense of subjective commitment, localizing it into a fetishized space. And for this reason, far from being 'incompatible' with Catholicism as Dupré suggests, Kierkegaard accords with the Catholic position *par excellence*. For example, as Aquinas says: 'the effect of a sacrament can be secured if it is received by desire, and not in fact' (*ST* III, q. 80, a.1, resp. 3). In other words, the disposition of the subject is absolutely central to the sacrament. Indeed, Aquinas implies that one need not receive the sacrament as such to receive its effects; one only has to desire it (although this still presupposes a sacrament rather than diminish the need for it).

What Kierkegaard fails to do, however, as Eller argues, is provide any 'detailed attention to sacramental theory' (Eller, 1968, p. 326), offering instead a number of works related to sacramental life. These are meant as aids, cultivating an existential commitment to the sacraments, imploring the communicant to give herself over totally to that which is communicated. That said one should not dismiss out of hand the value of a doctrinal approach for the very reasons Kierkegaard gives. Rather than make the usual claim that that practice has to be grounded in some sort of theory, one should argue as Herbert McCabe does, that doctrine is designed precisely to *prevent* oversimplification and misunderstandings (McCabe, 1999, p. 27). In other words, it is less about a positive description than about safeguarding what remains an unfathomable mystery. And this is Kierkegaard's point exactly: 'the speculative thinker explains the paradox [of Christ] in such a way that he cancels it' (CUP 227).

For this reason, in what follows I try to defend the doctrine of real presence on the basis that it maintains the constitutive trauma of Christ and thereby effects the shift to subjectivity, helping procure the subjective appropriation of truth: the assumption of desire.

Christ *is* the Eucharist

The initial basis for extending my thesis to the Eucharist is the Catholic affirmation that the Eucharist *is* Christ, a view attributed to the early Church (Pohle, 1909, p. 578), although only formally ratified by the Fourth Lateran Council (1215): 'His body and blood are truly contained in the sacrament of the altar under the forms of bread and wine' (Tanner, 1990, p. 230); reaffirmed at the Council of Trent (1545); and maintained in the *Catechism of the Catholic Church*: Christ is present *'in the Eucharistic species'* (*Catechism*, §1373; italics in original).

Of course, such continuity belies both the re-emergent disagreements that would have led in the first place to the need to re-ratify the doctrine over the course of history, and more specifically the way epistemological shifts mean that even though one council reaffirms the previous one, how that council understands the previous one may be different to how the previous council understood itself, a point I shall return to in a minute. For the moment, the evidence suggests as a bare minimum a continuity in terms of seeking to maintain the identity of Christ with those sacramental elements, an identity beyond that of remembrance, and hence the logical step in my own work from discussing Christ to discussing the Eucharist. How then does that which I have outlined about Christ translate into eucharistic terms?

Given the historical desire to maintain the identity of Christ with the sacramental elements of the Eucharist, it is possible to extend to the Eucharist that which has previously been maintained of Christ and Lacanian analysis. In short, the Eucharist, and in particular the point of transubstantiation, amounts to a form of analytic intervention which opens the historicity of the subject. I present my case through a sequence of six points which relate to the previous exposition of the analytic intervention in Chapter 8.

First, if Christ *is* the Eucharist one can qualify the relation of the divine and mundane in the terms already established, that is, the relation of eternity to time, or in Lacanese: the real to the symbolic. Christ's body manifests as the traumatic kernel of the bread, immanent to time yet that which refuses to be fully integrated into it. Indeed, one can defend this along the lines of Christology as defined by the Council of Chalcedon. On the one hand if the divine and the mundane are disjoined one would risk the eucharistic equivalent of the Nestorian heresy: impanation. The sacred host would be constituted in terms of two distinct and separate entities: the divine body of Christ covered in a separate wrap of bread. Consequently the Eucharist would lack the participatory quality. As Pickstock says, 'If the coincidence of the mystical and the real becomes fissured, the Eucharist signs . . . become . . . a matter of non-essential, *illustrative* signification which relies upon a non-participatory similitude between the bread and the Body' (Pickstock, 2000, p. 254; italics in original). On the other hand, the affirmation by Aquinas that the bread is not wholly taken up into the divine but retains its 'accidents' (*ST* III, q. 75, a. 5) precludes the eucharistic equivalent of the Monophysitic heresy. If the bread were wholly taken up into the divine then the Eucharist would fail to coincide with the historical temporality of the *ecclesia*. Instead, one should assert that Christ's body *is* the bread, distinct yet inextricably joined: Christ's body is the traumatic kernel of the bread as his blood is of the wine. Moreover, given this, it is possible to argue that any attempt to avoid testifying to Christ's presence in the Eucharist, such as that of the

Zwinglian reformers, or more recently the advocacy of the term 'transignification' (Schillebeeckx, 1968, p. 145), amount to a theological form of neurosis, a defence *against* the traumatic kernel of the real which is situated at the heart of the Eucharist: Christ's *real* presence.

This approach has already been suggested by Terry Eagleton, who notes that the basic tenet of Lacanian subjectivity is that, what founds a system cannot be represented within it because it is present only as the status of the real, the exception that grounds the event (Eagleton, 2002, pp. 513–17). Christ's institution of the Eucharist at the Last Supper gives birth to the event, yet he is subsequently hidden within the shape of the bread. Hence one can speak in Lacanian terms of the *real* presence of Christ in the Eucharist: Christ's flesh coincides with the bread as the traumatic kernel. Moreover, this would also constitute one way to read Aquinas' objection that the bread is bread as substance: 'by the power of God, who is the first cause of all things, it can come about that that which naturally follows on something else can still remain when that which is prior to it has been taken away' (*ST* III, q. 75, a. 3).

However, one should qualify this Lacanian scheme further. It is not that the real presence of Christ can be grasped only in terms of the failure of representation as Eagleton suggests (Eagleton, 2002, p. 517). Such an account would imply that the bread acts as a stand-in for the real of Christ who is rendered an unattainable object. Rather, in the Eucharist one encounters the real as bread, and this is why it is so traumatic. Here the split is not simply between symbolic reality and its inaccessible support, but inherent to the host itself, just as Christ is not a man transcendentally supported by God, Christ *is* God *and* man. Žižek expresses this point in terms of the difference between the 'real as impossible', where the real is unrefined and simply points to a failure of representation; and the 'impossible as real' (Žižek, 2004, p. 70), where the problem is precisely the obverse: that one *can* encounter the real (SXI 58). In theological terms this would constitute the difference between viewing grace as a kind of supernatural supplement, secretly sustaining the world;

or the very world itself in its mundane and material aspect as graced. In other words, we encounter God not as a mysterious addition that somehow evades us like an invisible force; rather we encounter God in life's very ordinariness. In a similar fashion, one can say that Christ is not God because of an extra-addition to his humanity; he is God because he is the first human who is fully human.[3]

At this point it is opportune to raise Graham Ward's criticism of the Lacanian real. His starting-point is our understanding of presence as it relates to the Eucharist. According to Ward, our modern understanding of presence is markedly different from the medieval accounts. In the modern period, under the influence of William of Ockham and Duns Scotus, 'what was given ontological priority and value was total presence, the transparency of a thing's self-existence, the self-grounded presentation of its complete meaning' (Ward, 2000, p. 169). That is to say, in the modern period presence is understood as a discrete entity, a localized and static property of an object's being. By contrast, earlier accounts of eucharistic presence were 'concerned with the nature of analogy' (Ward, 2000, p. 157). Presence was mediated and participated in God rather than being a self-sustained localized aspect of being. So with regard to the Eucharist, presence was understood in terms of the way the Eucharist 'rehearses the past, while drawing upon the futural expectations and significations of the act in the present' (Ward, 2000, p. 171). Ward argues that it was the modern construal of presence that became concurrent with Catholic belief at the Council of Trent, where it was employed to describe eucharistic presence. The modern rendition makes the shift towards the present as a localized space, rather than a participatory quality, an approach Ward considers idolatrous, 'reifying that which cannot be plucked out of time'; a fetishism of space (Ward, 2000, p. 159).[4] Commenting on Aquinas, Ward says:

---

3 I thank Conor Cunningham for our discussion and clarification of this point.

4 One could also argue that the two accounts of presence correspond to the difference between recollection and repetition. Recollection

[D]espite the ubiquitous use of the words present/presence/ real presence by translators, Aquinas does not employ that language in his account of sacramental realism . . . The language of *praesens* and *praesentia* only have reference to temporal and historical corporality and have to be understood analogically. (Ward, 2000, p. 157)

Indeed, Ward goes on to argue that Aquinas studiously avoided using such language with respect to 'Christ's giving of Himself in the Eucharist'; Aquinas talks about Christ existing in the sacrament, being 'really there (*vere esse*)', but not of presence (Ward, 2000, p. 158). For Aquinas, 'the sacrament while visibly present to the senses, celebrates the *anamnesis* of Christ's words in the upper room and looks forward to the beatific celebration to come' (Ward, 2000, p. 159).

How does this relate to Lacan? Ward argues that the Lacanian real is simply a negative version of the modern understanding of presence: 'what is prior is the negative version of full presence, the Void. That is the Real' (Ward, 2000, p. 169). In other words, Lacan's scheme simply reverses the modern terms of presence to indicate the ontological priority of lack. And crucially, because it is conceived by simply reversing the predicates of presence it is still governed by the logic of modernity; that is, it refuses participation. Thus from Ward's standpoint my Lacan is incompatible with the Eucharist.

However, if my own analysis is correct, Ward's critique may be a hasty conclusion for two reasons: first, as I have argued, Lacan has a strong psychoanalytical doctrine of *anamnesis* which is indebted to theological accounts; second, on the basis of Kierkegaard and Lacan I have argued that central to the process of *anamnesis* is the constitutive status of the real, the point of trauma which brings the tenses into relief. Without the antagonist kernel of the real, one is given to transcend time in

---

characterizes presence in modernity because it refuses time, it is localized and static like the truth to be discerned within. Repetition takes seriously the passage of becoming in time, and therefore construes presence in terms of participation.

the pursuit of objectivity which in turn undercuts the ability to talk meaningfully about time.

This leads me neatly on to my second main point regarding the relation of Christ to the Eucharist: if the trauma of Christ's initial intervention is, as Kierkegaard suggests, the condition of temporality, then Christ's repeated intervention in the form of the Eucharist ensures that time *remains* temporal. How precisely does the Eucharist ensure that time remains temporal? Through the institution of the Eucharist the subject is confronted by the traumatic presence of the eternal in time, the point of transubstantiation. In Kierkegaardian terms one could say this amounts to '*Øiblikket*', the blink of an eye, the Danish root of Heidegger's term *Augenblick*. Transubstantiation is the moment of intersection that both creates and bridges the past and future. And because the traumatic intervention brings the tenses into relief, the past is not simply trailing behind, lost over one's shoulder; rather, one can re-member it, as Jean-Luc Marion says, with 'eschatological patience' (Marion, 1991, p. 173). That is to say, one makes

an appeal, in the name of a past event, to God, in order that he recall an engagement (a covenant) that determines the instant presently given to the believing community . . . [T]he event remains less a past fact than a pledge given in the past in order, today still, to appeal to a future. (Marion, 1991, p. 172)

The present becomes figured between the past promise and future expectation. The present is not self-sufficient with regard to the past, but takes its meaning from the past, which comes back from the future. Hence the Eucharist becomes the paradigm for every present, constantly ensuring against the reification of 'now' as an eternal present by situating the subject in a dynamic and existential history, allowing the subject to be received into the fullness of time. The Catholic Church identifies this dynamic memorial as a process of *anamnesis* (*Catechism*, §1354). In Lacanian terms one could say that the point of transubstantiation amounts to a form of analytic intervention, which opens up the temporality of time. Indeed, it is only in neurosis that the subject is stuck in the '*hic et nunc*' (E 46/254) rather than open to the temporal flow. And because the subject is repeatedly exposed to the trauma of the Eucharist, he is invited into the constant process of reflection and affirmation, because each Sacred Mass is a chance to re-evaluate the signifiers that constitute identity in the light of Christ's incarnation, passion, resurrection and eschaton.

Third, the subject is not merely a passive observer; he is confronted by the sight of the host with the assertion that 'this is the body of Christ'. Is this not the perfect example of a humorous and indirect form of communication? It will be recalled that for Climacus humour is based upon a certain incongruity or contradiction between two images, as in the case of a caricature. As such, jokes were the perfect vehicle for Kierkegaard's attack on Hegel: jokes are a force of contradiction, and therefore resist the mediating sweep of rationality in which all opposites are sublated. On the basis of Lippitt's work I also suggested that a joke is a form of indirect communication because it avoids being a direct statement and demands interpretation, thereby fostering the subjective appropriation of truth.

I propose that one extend this framework to the Eucharist: the Eucharist is a bloody joke! Because just as Christ contains the contradiction of being *both* human *and* divine, the Eucharist offering of wine contains the contradiction that it is *both* wine *and* the blood of Christ. In the Eucharist one is faced with a paradox (the wine *is* the blood of Christ; the bread *is* the body of Christ) that refuses any form of mediation. Indeed, even the argument from tradition only testifies to a consistent belief in this paradox, not a rational explanation of that paradox. Instead the Eucharist calls for a Kierkegaardian leap into faith, a decisive interpretation and subjective appropriation of truth (CUP 93).

A similar point is made by Aquinas: 'We could never know by our senses that the real body of Christ and his blood are in the sacrament, but only by our faith' (*ST* III, q. 75, a. 1). In Lacanese, one could say that the Eucharist becomes a '*moment of concluding*' (E 48/257) because it hastens the interpretive decision we must make about the signifiers that determine us. Is this bread, or body, or both? Choosing the latter becomes a moment of self-criticism because it offers the chance to see oneself anew in the light of the Christian narrative; a narrative in which Christ's death and resurrection come back to us from the future as eschatological hope, calling us to decisive action in the present, freeing us from the burden of sin. The Christian narrative offers a different interpretation of one's life. Through that narrative one can see how one's life may be different. In the decisive moment of eucharistic intervention the subject is offered a glimpse at the way life can look from the other side of the Cross.

Fourth, the acceptance that the Eucharist contains the real presence of Christ helps stimulate a subjective appropriation of truth, what I have defined in Lacanian terms as the assumption of desire. The interpretive moment of concluding in which the subject, desiring God, chooses to accept the objective presence of Christ within the Eucharist, stimulates the contact of desire and will. The two are fused together through the interpretive decision in which the desire for God manifests with ritual enactment. And because the Eucharist encourages the assumption of desire, the case for the endless repetition of the Sacred Mass is presented. Eucharistic devotion constantly recalls us to live as Christians, existentially committed to Christ's saving Word.

Fifth, by giving ritual body to the concept of repetition, the Eucharist becomes the point *of* repetition. In his journal entries accompanying *Repetition*, Kierkegaard says that the highest expression of repetition is 'atonement' (R 320), the point at which we win ourselves back; and in *Repetition* this moment is described in terms of a bolt of thunder (R 212). Likewise, the Eucharist instigates the moment of repetition in that there is a traumatic point, the point of transubstantiation in which, like the bolt of thunder, the eternal coincides with time (indeed, this moment is usually accompanied by the clatter of boards or bells as if to signal the failure of language at this point). Yet this moment is also constitutive, co-extensive with winning oneself back because it is this point that invites a decisive interpretation. Through the interpretive moment of transubstantiation the past and future meet, temporality is opened up, and hence one enters the fullness of time. In that interpretive moment one repeats oneself, that is, reconstitutes oneself on the basis of a difference. Said otherwise, Kierkegaard's claim that 'Eternity is the true repetition' (R 221) can be read in terms of 'atonement' (R 320) because through the Eucharist one wins oneself back *anew* in the promise of eternal life.

Moreover, one should note how the Eucharist *is* repetition to the extent that the original event was established in time, and yet, as Catherine Pickstock argues, 'is continuous with its forward moving repetition, since the eternal "original" also exists in supplementing itself in an infinity without bounds' (Pickstock, 2000, p. 256). The Eucharist is a repetition in the sense that Christ's original identity is repeated through the difference that is every subsequent repetition. Repetition places Christ's identity in the Eucharist and this makes his identity a ceaseless task, 'incomplete' but not 'incoherent' (Pickstock, 2000, p. 266). This would constitute one way to account for the opposing claims that Christ's saving power was 'once and for all' (*Catechism*, §1364), and yet coterminous with the Eucharist; 'The sacrifice of Christ and the sacrifice of the Eucharist are *one single sacrifice*' (*Catechism*, §1367).

It also offers a different perspective on Kierkegaard's claim that 'Eternity is the true repetition' (R 221). Repetition is eternal because identity in repetition is *never* finalized. Indeed, only when the two statements are read together – repetition as 'winning oneself back' and repetition as an 'endless task' – can we maintain the proper tension in the concept.

On the Importance of the Eucharistic Context

Thus far I have considered the implication for understanding the Eucharist on the basis of analysis. In this section I argue that the ecclesial setting given by the Eucharist is also crucial for contextualizing both Kierkegaard and Lacan, and its wider political implications.

Turning to Kierkegaard first, one of the major contentions with his work is that it places too much emphasis on the individual at the expense of community. For example, Taylor argues that Kierkegaard fails to 'reintegrate . . . the self into the larger social-natural whole' (Taylor, 1975, p. 355). Similarly, Pickstock cites Climacus' plea: 'Every human being is too heavy for me, and therefore I plead . . .: let no one invite me, for I do not dance' (PF 8) to support her accusation that Kierkegaard encourages a 'covert individualism' (Pickstock, 2000, p. 272). It does not do to uncritically attribute Climacus' ideas to Kierkegaard; Climacus' refusal to dance may be indicative of *his* inability to commit himself to Christianity rather than Kierkegaard's individualism. Nonetheless, Pickstock's point reflects the institutional gap in Kierkegaard's work, the result of his reformed Lutheran background and distrust of the clergy. Indeed, Kierkegaard famously refused Holy Communion on his deathbed contending that it was not the reception of the sacrament as such he disdained, but its administration: he would happily receive it from a layman but not a priest (Grimsley, 1973, p. 110).

Perhaps Kierkegaard had anticipated the critique of his individualism when he suggested that unless the interpretive moment was ultimately referred to the eucharistic setting the question of atonement gets 'lost in the individual historical development' (CA 90). In other words, the interpretive moment is not simply about individual self-development because it only has meaning as part of the story of Christ's redemptive work, which is the story of the Church. And for this reason the Eucharist is the crucial context for his work.

Turning to Lacan, one should consider further Ward's critique. As he explains, the Eucharist repeats the crucifixion which 'effects a detachment, a distance' (Ward, 2000, p. 104). This in turn sets up an 'economy of desire experienced as mourning' (Ward, 2000, p. 104). Thus the Eucharist establishes a desire which invites one into the divine plenitude that constitutes the ongoing work of Christ. By contrast, for Lacan the origin of desire is lack, hence desire is always desire for a presence that never was and into which all returns. Thus at an ontological level redemption can mean little more than 'an emptying of oneself into nothingness (*à la Lacan*)' (Ward, 2000, p. 108). By contrast, eucharistic desire entails

> a recognition of the lack of foundation within oneself which requires and enables the reception of divine plenitude. Lacan returns the subject to the *nihilo* and denies that God made anything out of it. The Christian awareness of the absent body of Christ, and of death itself, returns us to our created-ness – to the giftedness of creation out of nothing. (Ward, 2000, p. 108)

The question arising at this point is the obvious one concerning the reception of the divine plenitude: does this not conform to the imaginary desire for wholeness? Is not the Eucharist merely an imaginary phallus to satiate the gap of the real rather than constitute an encounter with the real? Or, as Lacan would say: 'there is no Other of the other'. One should argue 'No' for two reasons: First, because subjective reflection unites action and desire so that the question of truth is no longer tied to reason but becomes embedded in endless striving. In a similar fashion, the endpoint of analysis is not constituted by the fulfilment *of* desire, but the point at which a space is opened where the subject is free to *pursue* desire, itself an endless task. Second, the introduction of divine plenitude does not overcome lack but reintroduces it, only now it is perceived from the perspective of plenitude rather than privation.

To illuminate this second point, consider Aquinas' distinction between the uses of ceremonial precepts – those acts that regulate worship – in the old and new law (i.e. Old and New Testaments). Aquinas introduces an analogy to illustrate the difference: 'Just as human reason fails to grasp the import of poetical utterance on account of its deficiency in truth, neither can it grasp divine things perfectly on account of their superabundance of truth' (*ST* I-II q. 101, a. 2, resp. 2). In other words, under the old law, sacrifice was necessary because of the lack of truth, that is, 'divine truth' had not been revealed through Christ; while in the new law ceremonial precepts are needed because the truth revealed through Christ is 'super-abundant [*excedentem*]'. It is as if through Christ's work the truth of God now shines so brightly in an ever unfolding and increasing measure that one needs the sacraments as a filter, like a pair of sunglasses, to funnel the divine radiance lest one should burn one's eyes. Here, lack is a product of the plenitude of God's truth; it is not that there is not enough, it is that there is too much! And herein is the difference between the respective goals of analysis and worship: in the former one must be reconciled to an ontological lack; in the latter lack is a sign of God's excessive love in which we share.

Finally, the political implications of an ecclesial and communal setting to analysis should not be lost. After all, as Elizabeth Danto has argued, far from being a Victorian practising in the closeted world of the female bourgeoisie, Freud was a modernist, a social activist caught up in the social democratic movement sweeping across Europe; and the newly discovered psychoanalysis was a crucial tool for social change. During the 1920s he and his first-wave colleagues envisaged a new kind of community based on free clinics, clinics committed to helping the poor and disenfranchised, cultivating good and productive individuals. Indeed, Anna Freud, Erik Erikson, and Wilhelm Reich all made psychoanalysis accessible to farmers, office clerks, teachers, domestic servants, public school teachers, and the like. But Freud's vision never took root, curtailed by a progression of policies that favoured private health care (Danto, 2005).

To this extent the Eucharist is in a unique position to respond because as William Cavanaugh has argued, politics is not a science of the given, but a practice of the imagination; that is, it establishes the conditions of possibilities for organizing bodies. The Eucharist is the privileged site of the Christian imagination, it offers alternative means to symbolically configure space, a different way of being with one another in the social sphere, and to that extent the Mass *is* political (Cavanaugh, 2003). In particular it has the power to challenge the private/public split that characterizes modern liberalism because the constitutive trauma and assumption of desire establishes the subject within an existing ecclesial setting. In contrast to the private clinic, liturgy does not ordain individuals with their own private set of desires or self-contained spheres of power (the critique of ego-psychology). Indeed, such an individual can only be imagined within the narrative construction of modern secular politics because only the secular conceives the individual as prior *to* society, and society merely a collection of pre-existing individuals with conflicting desires and competing interests. By contrast the ecclesial context of the Eucharist ensures a communal setting prior to the individual. Each individual is, before anything else, a member of the socially enacted body of Christ, a participatory member in a context that refuses still to allow the subject to be finalized, complete, or whole, because the self is a never-ending task, repeated forwards in the constant re-staging of the crucifixion, and beneficiary of love which always exceeds our capacity to understand. In other words, by situating analysis within the sociality of ecclesial worship Christianity is uniquely able to deliver on Freud's failed vision: to bring together the social and the private in the community, the necessary precondition of real therapy.

Such a view of the Eucharist should not be understood in terms of a necessary supplement to the harsh reality of secular pressures, but precisely an alternative site from which analytic methods can be developed into a form of collective analysis; where 'our daily bread is taken as a remedy against daily infirmity' (*ST* III, q. 79, a. 4); and a theological therapeutic by which analysis itself can become a form of worship because it is figured through the liturgical reception of the Eucharist. Put another way, after analysis one may look to the Church in its doctrinal, social, and performative functions to continually recreate through the Sacred Mass the conditions for the assumption of desire.

Moment of Concluding

In this work I have performed the retroactive reconfiguration of Lacan by way of Kierkegaard. Starting from Lacan, I have not merely shown the similarity between their respective projects, I have made the case that Lacan's return to Freud is really a return to Kierkegaard. In this sense I have performed a Lacanian intervention into the received view of his work, showing that it was Kierkegaard, not Freud, who was his predecessor. This allowed me to reconfigure Lacan along theological lines. Finally, I reflected on the Eucharist in the light of my theological reading of Lacan to suggest that if analysis is a parody of eucharistic intervention, then liturgy is properly speaking a theological therapeutic.

Reading Lacan on the basis of Kierkegaard has allowed me to unearth a very different Lacan to that usually championed by the postmodern philosophers of difference. They would have Lacan consign us to the flux in what at times may be taken as a neurotic fear against making a choice. Instead I have been able to situate Lacan within a tradition wherein recognizing one's temporality means taking seriously the question of how one is shaped by tradition; and a tradition for which a decisive choice is a constitutive and political act, rather than something to be endlessly deconstructed.

Reading Lacan through Kierkegaard has been a coterminous process of reading Kierkegaard through Lacan. This has allowed me not only to affirm some traditional Kierkegaardian scholarship with regard to the depiction of the stages, the use of pseudonyms, indirect communication, and his thesis that truth is subjectivity, but also to articulate them anew through Lacan's categories. This gives freshness to Kierkegaardian studies, making Kierkegaard contemporary for postmodernity. At the same time I have challenged much of the literature that has previously dealt with Kierkegaard from a psychoanalytic perspective, arguing that it is not ego-psychology he anticipates, but Lacanian psychoanalysis. In a similar fashion, in the final chapter I have been able to show the value of Lacan's work in defending an orthodox Catholic or indeed high Anglican approach to the Eucharist, which stresses transubstantiation. I have found a new language to talk about the Eucharist, thereby building bridges between the disciplines of theology and psychoanalysis.

Through a Kierkegaardian engagement with Lacan this work articulates the theoretical underpinning to interventions, both psychoanalytical and theological. This approach can be seen to correspond to Augustine's vision of a city of God. The city of God is not another city in the geographical sense, nor is it located in the afterlife; it is, as Milbank says, the city of man 'interrupted by another beginning' (Milbank, 1993, p. 391), a city based upon and participating in the worship of the one true God. This work not only articulates the means of those interruptions, it performs one such interruption into Lacanian analysis.

I end with a reflection on the concluding stanzas of the last canto of Dante's *Paradiso*. At the end of his journey, from the dark forest, through the realms of Hell, Purgatory, and Paradise, Dante glimpses the Trinity only to struggle with the comprehension. Finally he says:

ma non eran da ciò le proprie penne
se non che la mia mente fu percossa
da un fulgore in che sua voglia venne

A l'alta fantasia qui mancò possa;
ma già volgeva il mio disio e'l velle,
sí come rota ch'igualmente è mossa
l'amor che move il sole e l'altre stelle.

[But that was not a flight for my wings:
Except that my mind was struck by a flash
In which what it willed [*voglia*] came to it.

At this point high imagination failed;
But already my desire [*disio*] and my will
Were being turned like a wheel, all at one speed.
Love moves the sun and other stars.]

(Canto XXXIII, 139–44)

Why should Dante's 'imagination fail'? According to the standard reading, the stress on the imagination's failure emphasizes the passivity of the will. It is, as William James might say, as if one's own will was in abeyance, such that one is 'held by a superior power' (James, 1909, p. 381). And indeed, James cites passivity as one of the four fundamental features of a religious experience. However, perhaps an alternative reading is possible, which would affirm my own argument? What brings out the imagination's failure is not the passivity of the will, but its very opposite: the activity of the will, that is, the fact that the will is now engaged, with desire through action, turning as Dante suggests 'at one speed'. In Kierkegaardian terms, if Dante is not creatively thinking about God, it is not because God has suddenly appeared in full splendour before him rendering him speechless, but because Dante embodies the God relation in his incarnate action which unites desire for God with will.

But notice how the imagination's failure is precipitated by the vision of the Trinity: 'my mind was struck by a flash'. Likewise, the Eucharist is taken in the context of having affirmed the Trinity. At the highpoint of the Mass, is the eucharistic intervention, whereby the bread and wine are struck by a flash as the eternal Son coincides with the temporal realm (signalled by the bells). In this moment our desire for God is matched by God's desire for us. The Eucharist creates the conditions for the assumption of desire: the contradiction contained therein forces the earnestness of faith; one must leave behind the shared comfort of reason for the 'madness' (CUP 194) of Christianity and in doing so become subjectively engaged in eucharistic practice. The point at which we both approach the altar and partake of Christ's body and blood is the point desire and will turn at 'one speed'. Imagination fails not because one is lost, caught up in the seventh heaven, but because the question of Christianity – what it means to live and experience God's love or to live a life of risk in Christ – is now seen principally in terms of engaged and embodied action: the assumption of desire. This is the point at which, after analysis, the analysand is delivered over to doxology.

Bibliography

Aquinas, Thomas, 1964–81, *Summa Theologiae*, 61 vols, London and New York: Blackfriars.
—— 1975, *Summa Contra Gentiles*, vol. 1, trans. Anton C. Pegis, Notre Dame and London: University of Notre Dame Press.
Arbaugh, George E. and George B. Arbaugh, 1968, *Kierkegaard's Authorship*, London: George Allen & Unwin.
Aristotle, 1984, *The Complete Works of Aristotle: The Revised Oxford Translation*, ed. Jonathan Barnes, Princeton, N.J.: Princeton University Press.
Auden, W. H., 1940, *Another Time*, London: Random House.
Augustine, 1950, *The Greatness of the Soul/The Teacher*, trans. J. Colleran, Westminster: Newman Press.

Ballard, P., 2000, 'The emergence of pastoral and practical theology in Britain', in *The Blackwell Reader in Pastoral and Practical Theology*, ed. J. Woodward and S. Pattison, Oxford: Blackwell.
Barret, Lee, 1985, 'Kierkegaard's "*Anxiety*" and the Augustinian doctrine of original sin', in *The Concept of Anxiety*, ed. Robert Perkins, International Kierkegaard Commentary, 8, Georgia: Mercer University Press.
Becker, Ernest, 1997, *The Denial of Death*, New York: Free Press.
Beira, Mario L., 2000, 'Reflections on Lacan's view of interpretation', in *The Subject of Lacan*, ed. Kareen Malone and Stephen Friedlander, Albany: SUNY Press.
Bettelheim, Bruno, 1986, *Surviving the Holocaust*, London: Flamingo.
Blum, Harold P., 1998, 'Ego-psychology and contemporary structural theory', *International Psychoanalysis* 2. http://www.ipa.org.uk/newsletter/98-2/blum.1.htm
Boothby, Richard, 2001, *Freud as Philosopher: Metapsychology after Lacan*, New York and London: Routledge.
Brousse, Marie-Hélène, 1995, 'The Drive (II)', in *Reading Seminar XI: Lacan's Four Fundamental Concepts of Psychoanalysis*, ed. Richard Feldstein, Bruce Fink and Maire Jaanus, Albany: SUNY Press.

Bibliography

Butler, Rex, 2005, *Slavoj Žižek, Live Theory*, New York and London: Continuum.

Caputo, John, 1987, *Radical Hermeneutics: Repetition, Deconstruction, and the Hermeneutic Project*, Bloomington: Indiana University Press.

Caruth, Cathy, 1996, *Unclaimed Experience: Trauma, Narrative, and History*, Baltimore and London: Johns Hopkins University Press.

Cavanaugh, William, 2003, *The Theopolitical Imagination*, Edinburgh: T&T Clark.

Clément, C., 1983, *The Lives and Legends of Jacques Lacan*, trans. Arthur Goldhammer, New York: Columbia University Press.

Cloeren, Hermann, 1985, 'The linguistic turn in Kierkegaard's attack on Hegel', *International Studies in Philosophy* 17, 1–13.

Cole, Preston, 1971, *The Problematic Self in Kierkegaard and Freud*, New Haven and London: Yale University Press.

Coward, H., and Foshay, T., eds, 1992, *Derrida and Negative Theology*, Albany: SUNY Press.

Cross, F. L., ed., 1957, *The Oxford Dictionary of the Christian Church*, London: Oxford University Press.

Crownfield, David, 1989, 'Extraduction', in *Lacan and Theological Discourse*, ed. Edith Wyschogrod, David Crownfield and Carl Raschke, Albany: SUNY Press.

Cunningham, Conor, 2002, *Genealogy of Nihilism*, London and New York: Routledge.

Danto, Elizabeth, 2005, *Freud's Free Clinic: Psychoanalysis and Social Justice, 1918–1938*, New York: Columbia University Press.

Dawe, R. H., 1968, 'Some Reflections on *Até* and *Hamartia*', *Harvard Studies in Classical Philology* 72, 89–124.

de Lubac, Henri, 1997, 'Spiritual understanding', trans. Luke O'Neill, in *The Theological Interpretation of Scripture: Classic and Contemporary Readings*, ed. Stephen Fowl, Oxford: Blackwell.

Derrida, J., 1992, 'How to avoid speaking: denials', in *Derrida and Negative Theology*, ed. Harold Coward and Toby Foshay, Albany: SUNY Press.

Dodds, E. R., 1953, *The Greeks and the Irrational*, Berkeley: University of California Press.

Doyle, R., ed., 1984, *Ate, its Uses and Meaning: A Study in the Greek Poetic Tradition from Homer to Euripides*, New York: Fordham University Press.

Dreyfus, Hubert L., 1991, *Being-in-the-World*, Massachusetts: MIT Press.

Dupré, Louis, 1963, *Kierkegaard as Theologian*, New York: Sheed & Ward.

—— 1985, 'Of time and eternity', in *The Concept of Anxiety*, ed. Robert Perkins, International Kierkegaard Commentary, 8, Macon, Ga.: Mercer University Press.

Eagleton, Terry, 2002, 'Irony and the Eucharist', *New Blackfriars* 981, 513–17.

Eco, Umberto, 1984, *Semiotics and the Philosophy of Language*, London: Macmillan.

Eller, Vernard, 1968, *Kierkegaard and Radical Discipleship: A New Perspective*, Princeton, N.J.: Princeton University Press.

Elrod, John, 1975, *Being and Existence in Kierkegaard's Pseudonymous Works*, Princeton, N.J.: Princeton University Press.

Erikson, Erik, 1959, 'Ego development and historical change', *Psychological Issues* 1, 18–49.

Evans, C. Stephen, 1983, *Kierkegaard's 'Fragments' and 'Postscript': The Religious Philosophy of Johannes Climacus*, Atlantic Highlands: Humanities Press.

Evans, Dylan, 1996, *An Introductory Dictionary of Lacanian Psychoanalysis*, London and New York: Routledge.

Fabro, C., 1980, 'Analogy', in *Bibliotheca Kierkegaardiana*, vol. 5, ed. Niels Thulstrup and Marie Thulstrup, Copenhagen: Reitzels.

Farrell, Kirby, 1998, *Post-Traumatic Culture: Injury and Interpretation in the Nineties*, Baltimore and London: Johns Hopkins University Press.

Ferguson, Duncan S., 1986, *Biblical Hermeneutics: An Introduction*, London: John Knox Press.

Fink, Bruce, 1995, *The Lacanian Subject: Between Language and Jouissance*, Princeton, N.J.: Princeton University Press.

—— 2000, *A Clinical Introduction to Lacanian Psychoanalysis: Theory and Technique*, London: Harvard University Press.

Flannery, Austin, ed., 1982, *Vatican Council II: More Postconciliar Documents*, New York: Costello.

Forsyth, James, 1997, *Faith and Human Transformation: A Dialogue between Psychology and Theology*, Lanham, Md.: University Press of America.

Freud, Anne, 1936, *The Ego and the Mechanisms of Defence*, London: Hogarth Press.

—— 1966, *Normality and Pathology in Childhood*, London: Hogarth Press.

Freud, S. All references are to the *Standard Edition of the Complete Psychological Works of Freud*, 24 vols, ed. and trans. James Strachey, in collaboration with Anna Freud, assisted by Alix Strachey and Alan Tyson, London: Hogarth Press, 1953–74.

—— 'Analysis of a phobia in a five-year-old boy' (1909), vol. 10, pp. 3–150.

—— 'Analysis terminable and interminable' (1937), vol. 23, pp. 209–55.

—— *Beyond the Pleasure Principle* (1920), vol. 18, pp. 1–64.

—— *Civilisation and its Discontents* (1930 [1929]), vol. 21, pp. 57–146.

—— *The Interpretation of Dreams* (1900), vol. 4.

—— *Jokes and their Relation to the Unconscious* (1905), vol. 8.

—— *Moses and Monotheism* (1939), vol. 23, pp. 1–139.

—— 'The neuro-psychoses of defence' (1894), vol. 3, pp. 41–62.

—— 'A note on the unconscious in psychoanalysis' (1912), vol. 12, pp. 255–66.

—— 'Notes upon a case of obsessional neurosis' (1909), vol. 10, pp. 151–318.

—— *An Outline of Psycho-Analysis* (1940 [1938]), vol. 23, pp. 139–208.

—— 'Project for a scientific psychology' (1895), vol. 1, pp. 281–387.

—— 'Psycho-analytic notes on an autobiographical account of a case of paranoia (*dementia paranoides*)' (1911), vol. 12, pp. 1–80.

—— 'The psychogenesis of a case of homosexuality in a woman' (1920), vol. 18, pp. 145–72.

—— 'Recommendations to physicians practising psycho-analysis' (1912), vol. 12, pp. 109–20.

—— 'Remembering, repeating and working-through' (1914), vol. 12, pp. 145–56.

—— *Totem and Taboo* (1913 [1912–13]), vol. 13, pp. 1–162.

Friedmann, Rudolph, 1949, *Kierkegaard: The Analysis of the Psychological Personality*, London: Peter Nevill.

Garff, Joakim, 2005, *Søren Kierkegaard: A Biography*, trans. Bruce Kirmmse, Princeton and Oxford: Princeton University Press.

Goppelt, Leonhard, 1982, *Typos: The Typological Interpretation of the Old Testament in the New*, trans. Donald H. Madvig, Michigan: Eerdmans.

Goscinny, René, and Albert Uderzo, 1974, *Asterix and the Big Fight*, trans. Anthea Bell and Derek Hockridge, London: Hodder Children's Books.

Grimsley, Ronald, 1973, *Søren Kierkegaard: A Biographical Introduction*, London: Studio Vista.

Hale, Geoffrey, 2002, *Kierkegaard and the Ends of Language*, Minneapolis and London: University of Minnesota Press.

Hall, Amy Laura, 2002, *Kierkegaard and the Treachery of Love*, Cambridge: Cambridge University Press.

Hamann, Johann Georg, 1949–57, *Sämtliche Werke, historisch-kritische Ausgabe*, vol. 3, ed. Josef Nadler, Vienna: Herder.

Bibliography

Hegel, Georg, 1977, *Phenomenology of Spirit*, trans. A. V. Miller, Oxford: Oxford University Press.

Heidegger, Martin, 1962, *Being and Time*, trans. John Macquarrie and Edward Robinson, Southampton: Blackwell.

Herbermann, Charles, *et al.*, eds, 1907–22, *The Catholic Encyclopedia*, London: Caxton.

Hill, Philip, 2002, *Using Lacanian Clinical Technique: An Introduction*, London: Press for the Habilitation of Psychoanalysis.

Hughes, J., 1912, 'Ubiquitarians', in *The Catholic Encyclopedia*, vol. 15, ed. Charles Herbermann *et al.*, London: Caxton.

Jakobson, Roman, 1987, 'Two aspects of language and two types of aphasic disturbances', in *Language and Literature*, ed. Krystyna Pomorska, Cambridge Mass., and London: Harvard University Press.

James, William, 1909, *The Varieties of Religious Experience: A Study in Human Nature*, London: Longmans, Green & Co.

Johnson, Richard, 1999, 'MacIntyre, Kierkegaard and the Post-Metaphysical Critique of Rational Theology', unpublished doctoral thesis, Bristol University.

Kant, Immanuel, 1979, *The Conflict of the Faculties*, trans M. J. Gregor, New York: Abaris.

Kay, Sarah, 2003, *Žižek: A Critical Introduction*, Cambridge: Polity Press.

Kierkegaard, Søren, 1941, *For Self-Examination/Judge for Yourselves/ Three Discourses*, trans. Walter Lowrie, London: Oxford University Press.

—— 1950, *Edifying Discourse*, Augsburg.

—— 1958a, *Johannes Climacus*, trans. T. H. Croxall, London: Adam & Charles Black.

—— 1958b, *The Journals of Kierkegaard, 1834–1854*, ed. and trans. Alexander Dru, London: Fontana.

—— 1967, *Journals and papers*, vols 1–6, ed. and trans. Howard V. Hong and Edna H. Hong, Princeton, N.J.: Princeton University Press.

—— 1972, *Training in Christianity*, trans. Walter Lowrie, Princeton, N.J.: Princeton University Press.

—— 1978, *Two Ages: The Age of Revolution and the Present Age/A Literary Review*, ed. and trans. Howard V. Hong and Edna H. Hong, Princeton, N.J.: Princeton University Press.

—— 1980, *The Concept of Anxiety*, ed. and trans. Reidar Thormte and Albert B. Anderson, Princeton, N.J.: Princeton University Press.

—— 1980, *The Sickness Unto Death: A Christian Psychological Exposition for Upbuilding and Awakening*, ed. and trans. Howard V. Hong and Edna H. Hong, Princeton, N.J.: Princeton University Press.

—— 1983, *Fear and Trembling*, ed. and trans. Howard V. Hong and Edna H. Hong, Princeton, N.J.: Princeton University Press.

—— 1983, *Repetition*, ed. and trans. Howard V. Hong and Edna H. Hong, Princeton, N.J.: Princeton University Press.

—— 1985, *Johannes Climacus*, ed. and trans. Howard V. Hong and Edna H. Hong, Princeton, N.J.: Princeton University Press.

—— 1985, *Philosophical Fragments*, ed. and trans. Howard V. Hong and Edna H. Hong, Princeton, N.J.: Princeton University Press.

—— 1987, *Either/Or*, vols 1 and 2, ed. and trans. Howard V. Hong and Edna H. Hong, Princeton, N.J.: Princeton University Press.

—— 1988, *Stages on Life's Way*, ed. and trans. Howard V. Hong and Edna H. Hong, Princeton, N.J.: Princeton University Press.

—— 1992, *Concluding Unscientific Postscript to Philosophical Fragments*, vols 1 and 2, ed. and trans. Howard V. Hong and Edna H. Hong, Princeton, N.J.: Princeton University Press.

—— 1995, *Works of Love*, ed. and trans. Howard V. Hong and Edna H. Hong, Princeton, N.J.: Princeton University Press.

—— 1998, *Armed Neutrality*, ed. and trans. Howard V. Hong and Edna H. Hong, Princeton, N.J.: Princeton University Press.

—— 1998, 'On my work as an author', in *The Point of View*, ed. and trans. Howard V. Hong and Edna H. Hong, Princeton, N.J.: Princeton University Press.

—— 1998, *The Point of View/Armed Neutrality*, ed. and trans. Howard V. Hong and Edna H. Hong, Princeton, N.J.: Princeton University Press.

Kojève, Alexandre, 1969, *Introduction to the Reading of Hegel*, ed. Allan Bloom, trans. James H. Nichols, Jr, London: Basic Books.

Kristeva, Julia, 1987, *In the Beginning was Love: Psychoanalysis and Faith*, trans. Arthur Goldhammer, New York: Columbia University Press.

—— 1997, *The Portable Kristeva*, ed. Kelly Oliver, New York: Columbia University Press.

Lacan, Jacques, 1966, *Écrits*, Paris: Seuil.

—— 2002, *Écrits: A Selection*, trans. Bruce Fink, New York and London: W. W. Norton & Company.

—— 1981, *The Language of the Self: The Function of Language in Psychoanalysis* (1953), trans. Anthony Wilden, London: Johns Hopkins University Press.

—— 1995, 'Position of the unconscious' (1966), trans. Bruce Fink, in *Reading Seminar XI: Lacan's Four Fundamental Concepts of Psychoanalysis*, ed. Richard Feldstein, Bruce Fink, and Maire Jaanus, Albany: SUNY Press.

—— 1991, *The Seminar of Jacques Lacan, I: Freud's Papers on Tech-*

Bibliography

nique, 1953–1954, ed. Jacques-Alain Miller, trans. John Forrester, London and New York: W. W. Norton & Company.

—— 1991, *The Seminar of Jacques Lacan, II: The Ego in Freud's Theory and in the Technique of Psychoanalysis, 1954–1955*, ed. Jacques-Alain Miller, trans. Sylvana Tomaselli, London and New York: W. W. Norton & Company.

—— 2000, *The Seminar of Jacques Lacan, III: The Psychoses, 1955–1956*, ed. Jacques-Alain Miller, trans. Russell Grigg, London: Routledge.

—— *The Seminar of Jacques Lacan: The Formations of the Unconscious, 1957–1958*, trans. Cormac Gallagher, unpublished.

—— 1992, *The Seminar of Jacques Lacan, VII: The Ethics of Psychoanalysis, 1959–1960*, ed. Jacques-Alain Miller, trans. Dennis Porter, London: Routledge.

—— 1991, *Le Séminaire Livre VIII: Le Transfert* (1960–1), ed. Jacques-Alain Miller, Paris: Seuil.

—— 1998, *The Seminar of Jacques Lacan, XI: The Four Fundamental Concepts of Psycho-analysis* (1964), ed. Jacques-Alain Miller, trans. Alan Sheridan, London: Vintage.

—— 1998, *The Seminar of Jacques Lacan, XX: On Feminine Sexuality: The Limits of Love and Knowledge, 1972–1973*, ed. Jacques-Alain Miller, trans. Bruce Fink, London and New York: W. W. Norton & Company

Lake, Frank, 1966, *Clinical Theology: A Theological and Psychiatric Basis to Clinical Pastoral Care*, London: Darton, Longman & Todd.

Laplanche, Jean, and Jean-Bertrand Pontalis, 1988, *The Language of Psychoanalysis*, London: Karnac.

Lee, Jonathan Scott, 1990, *Jacques Lacan*, Boston: Twayne.

Lévi-Strauss, Claude, 1963, *Structural Anthropology*, trans. Claire Jacobson and Brooke Grundfest Schoepf, London: Basic Books.

—— 1969, *The Elementary Structures of Kinship*, trans. James Harle Bell, John Richard von Sturmer and Rodney Needham, London: Eyre & Spottiswoode.

Lippitt, John, 2000, *Humour and Irony in Kierkegaard's Thought*, London: Macmillan.

—— 2003, *Kierkegaard and Fear and Trembling*, London and New York: Routledge.

Loewald, Hans, 1971, 'Some considerations on repetition and repetition compulsion', *International Journal of Psycho-Analysis* 52, 59–65.

Lyotard, Jean-François, 1983, 'The dream-work does not think', *Oxford Literary Review* 1, 3–34.

Maas, A. J., 1912, 'Communicatio idiomatum', in *The Catholic Encyclopedia*, vol. 4, ed. Charles Herbermann *et al.*, London, Caxton.

Macey, David, 1988, *Lacan in Contexts*, London: Verso.

Mackey, Louis, 1984, 'Once more with feeling: Kierkegaard's repetition', in *Kierkegaard and Literature: Irony, Repetition, and Criticism*, ed. Ronald Schleifer and Robert Markley, Oklahoma: University of Oklahoma Press.

McCabe, Herbert, 1999, 'The Eucharist as language', in *Catholicism and Catholicity: Eucharistic Communities in Historical and Contemporary Perspectives*, ed. Sara Beckwith, Oxford: Blackwell.

MacIntyre, A., 1999, *After Virtue: A Study in Moral Theory*, 2nd edn, London: Duckworth.

McTaggart, John Ellis, 2001, 'Time', in *Metaphysics: Contemporary Readings*, ed. Michael J. Loux, London and New York: Routledge.

Magurshak, Dan, 1985, '*The Concept of Anxiety*: the keystone of the Kierkegaard-Heidegger relationship', in *The Concept of Anxiety*, International Kierkegaard Commentary, 8, ed. Robert L. Perkins, Macon, Ga.: Mercer University Press.

Marion, Jean-Luc, 1991, *God Without Being*, trans. Thomas A. Carlson, Chicago: University of Chicago Press.

Milbank, John, 1993, *Theology and Social Theory: Beyond Secular Reason*, Oxford: Blackwell.

—— 1998a, 'The sublime in Kierkegaard', in *Post-Secular Philosophy: Between Philosophy and Theology*, ed. Phillip Blond, London and New York: Routledge.

—— 1998b, *The Word Made Strange: Theology, Language, Culture*, Oxford: Blackwell.

—— 2003, *Being Reconciled: Ontology and Pardon*, London and New York: Routledge.

Milbank, John, and Catherine Pickstock, 2001, *Truth in Aquinas*, London: Routledge.

Nobus, Dany, 2000, *Jacques Lacan and the Freudian Practice of Psycho-analysis*, London and Philadelphia: Routledge.

Nordentoft, Kresten, 1978, *Kierkegaard's Psychology*, trans. Bruce H. Kirmmse, Pittsburgh: Duquesne University Press.

Origen, 1979, *On First Principles: Book IV*, in *Origen*, trans. Rowan A. Greer, London: SPCK.

Patterson, George, 2002, *Kierkegaard, Religion and the Nineteenth-Century Crisis of Culture*, Cambridge: Cambridge University Press.

Peuser, Gunter, 1987, 'Jargonaphasia and schizophasis: an essay in contrastive patholinguistics', in *Neurotic and Psychotic Language Behaviour*, ed. R. Wodak and P. Van de Craen, Clevedon: Multilingual Matters.

Phillips, Adam, 1995, *Terrors and Experts*, London: Faber & Faber.

Pickstock, Catherine, 2000, *After Writing: On the Liturgical Consummation of Philosophy*, Oxford: Blackwell.

Plato, 1981, *Meno*, trans. W. K. C. Guthrie, Harmondsworth: Penguin.

Pohle, J., 1909, 'Eucharist', in *The Catholic Encyclopedia*, vol. 5, ed. Charles Herbermann *et al.*, London: Caxton.

Pound, M., 2005, 'Having a good time with Kierkegaard: McTaggart, Kierkegaard, and the ethical status of time', *Philosophical Writings* 28, 13–22.

Rae, Murray A., 1997, *Kierkegaard's Vision of the Incarnation: By Faith Transformed*, Oxford: Clarendon Press.

Rapaport, David, 1959, 'A historical survey of psychoanalytic ego-psychology', *Psychological Issues* 1, 5–17.

Rasmussen, R., 2005, 'Kill me a son: on Kierkegaard and Lacan', *Psychoanalytic Notebooks* 14, 110–16.

Richardson, W., 1986, 'Psychoanalysis and the God question', *Thought* 61, 68–83.

—— 1997, '"Like straw": religion and psychoanalysis', *The Letter: Lacanian Perspectives on Psychoanalysis* 11, 1–15.

Roazen, Paul, 1996, 'Lacan's first disciple', *Journal of Religious Health* 4, 321–36, 324.

Rose, Gillian, 1992, *The Broken Middle*, Oxford: Blackwell.

Roudinesco, Elizabeth, 1990, *Jacques Lacan & Co.: A History of Psychoanalysis in France, 1925–1985*, trans. Jeffrey Mehlman, Chicago: University of Chicago Press.

—— 1999, *Jacques Lacan: An Outline of a Life and a History of a Thought*, trans. Barbara Bray, Cambridge: Polity Press.

Safouan, Moustapha, 2000, *Jacques Lacan and the Question of Psychoanalytic Training*, trans. Jacqueline Rose, London: MacMillan.

Saussure, Ferdinand de, 1974, *Course in General Linguistics*, trans. Wade Baskin, Glasgow: Fontana and Collins.

Schillebeeckx, Edward, 1968, *The Eucharist*, New York: Sheed & Ward.

Schmitt, Carl, 1985, *Political Theology: Four Chapters on the Concept of Sovereignty*, trans. G. Schwab, Cambridge, Mass.: MIT Press.

Shakespeare, Steven, 2001, *Kierkegaard, Language and the Reality of God*, Aldershot: Ashgate.

Sophocles, 1972, *The Theban Plays*, trans. E. F. Watling, London: Penguin.

Stack, George, 1977, *Kierkegaard's Existential Ethics*, Alabama: University of Alabama Press.

Tanner, Norman, ed., 1990, *Decrees of the Ecumenical Councils*, 2 vols, London: Sheed & Ward.

Bibliography

Taylor, Mark C., 1975, *Kierkegaard's Pseudonymous Authorship: A Study of Time and the Self*, Princeton, N.J.: Princeton University Press.
—— 1980, *Journeys to Selfhood: Hegel and Kierkegaard*, London: University of California Press.
—— 1984, *Erring: A Postmodern A/Theology*, London: University of Chicago Press.
—— 1989, 'Refusal of the Bar', in *Lacan and Theological Discourse*, ed. Edith Wyschogrod, David Crownfield, and Carl Raschke, Albany: SUNY Press.
Thompson, Josiah, 1967, *The Lonely Labyrinth: Kierkegaard's Pseudonymous Works*, London and Amsterdam: Southern Illinois University Press.

Walker, Jeremy, 1985, *The Descent into God*, Montreal: McGill-Queen's University Press.
Ward, Graham, 2000, *Cities of God*, London and New York: Routledge.
Winquist, Charles, 1989, 'Lacan and theological discourse', in *Lacan and Theological Discourse*, ed. Edith Wyschogrod, David Crownfield, and Carl Raschke, Albany: SUNY Press.
—— 1998, 'Lacan and theology', in *Post-Secular Philosophy*, ed. Phillip Blond, London and New York: Routledge.
Wyschogrod, Edith, Crownfield, D. and Raschke, C., eds, 1989, *Lacan and Theological Discourse*, Albany: SUNY Press.
Wyschogrod, Michael, 1954, *Kierkegaard and Heidegger: The Ontology of Existence*, London: Routledge.

Žižek, S., 1996, *The Indivisible Remainder: An Essay on Schelling and Related Matters*, London and New York: Verso.
—— 2000a, *The Fragile Absolute: Or, Why is the Christian Legacy Worth Fighting For?* London and New York: Verso.
—— 2000b, *The Ticklish Subject: The Absent Centre of Political Ontology*, London and New York: Verso.
—— 2001, *Enjoy Your Symptom: Jacques Lacan in Hollywood and Out*, 2nd edn, London and New York: Routledge.
—— 2002, *The Sublime Object of Ideology*, London and New York: Verso.
Žižek, S., and Glyn Daly, 2004, *Conversations with Žižek*, Cambridge: Polity Press.

Index of Names and Subjects